Management for Profes

The Springer series *Management for Professionals* comprises high-level business and management books for executives. The authors are experienced business professionals and renowned professors who combine scientific background, best practice, and entrepreneurial vision to provide powerful insights into how to achieve business excellence.

More information about this series at http://www.springer.com/series/10101

Ondrej Zizlavsky • Eddie Fisher

Innovation Scorecard

A Method to Measure Innovation in
Agile Projects and Business
Environments

Ondrej Zizlavsky
Faculty of Business and Management
Brno University of Technology
Brno, Czech Republic

Eddie Fisher
SKEMA Business School
Euralille, France

ISSN 2192-8096 ISSN 2192-810X (electronic)
Management for Professionals
ISBN 978-3-030-82690-1 ISBN 978-3-030-82688-8 (eBook)
https://doi.org/10.1007/978-3-030-82688-8

This Springer imprint is published by the registered company Springer Nature Switzerland AG.
The registered company address is: Gewerbestrasse 11, 6330 Cham, Switzerland

Preface

Most people would agree that the management of innovation in areas such as agile projects and other work environments is of topical interest to many businesses. It appears that innovation strategy is delivered through the appropriate application of project and management and other management approaches. But how do we know how successful any innovation has been? What has been missing is a sound approach to manage the efficiency and effectiveness of measuring how successful innovations or changes in (agile) projects and other work environments have been. In the past, practitioners made good use of available measurement models such as the balanced scorecard (Kaplan & Norton, 1996).

Welcome to the Innovation Scorecard

The purpose of this guide is to allow us to share with you many ideas, methods, and techniques that—irrespective of the industry you operate within, or your geographical work location—will enable you to put these to practice, having first been made familiar with the associated theories that underpin our practical solutions. Constant learning and practice in this relatively new area of performance management is essential for those who wish to widen and improve their 'measuring success' skills. We are certain that you will become more successful in your future endeavours.

An effective innovation performance measurement system or methodology must be specifically designed for work activities that relate to the measurement of how successful an innovation has been. Such a system needs to include appropriate and user-friendly metrics that allow for the measurement of innovation within projects/initiatives irrespective of the kind and type of work that is being managed. When applied appropriately and in accordance with existing company strategy, marketing drives, and HR/corporate policies, processes, and procedures, innovation metrics provide managers and employees with opportunities to 'plan, organise, monitor, and control' the success of all innovation activities for the benefit of the organisation they work for.

Only by Learning. Success by Practice

How will you benefit from the information and the presented details contained within these guidelines? Our guide aims to close the identified gap in the current practice of how to measure the success in (agile) innovation projects/initiatives and other work environments and to provide easy to follow and clear end-to-end steps on how to achieve this. The suggested innovation scorecard methodology acts as a 'one-stop shop' and provides project and business managers with the tools, techniques, worked samples, and associated templates to start the journey of measuring the level of success of any innovation or change. As we present the many ideas (Part I—Theory), we will share various methods and techniques that will help you to put our thoughts to practice (Part II—Practice) to achieve maximum benefit. There will be copious examples of how our ideas can be applied in real-life practical work environments. We suggest that you customise our suggested ideas to your own activities, to your own style, and to you!

The authors confirm that the 'proof of concept' is based on actual applications in a real live ongoing project in the Czech Republic (three sub-projects) in agile software development. The third of these considered case studies engaged in activities relating to business development and operational issues. This strengthens the authors' claim that the innovation scorecard methodology can be applied irrespective of the work environment or its geography.

Reference
Kaplan, R. S., & Norton, D. P. (1996). *The balanced scorecard: Translating strategy into action*. Harvard Business School Press.

Brno, Czech Republic   Ondrej Zizlavsky
Euralille, France   Eddie Fisher

Acknowledgements

Many people and organisations have helped us to produce these guidelines. We are delighted to thank them all, in particular:

This guide is the result of work undertaken on behalf of the Technology Agency of the Czech Republic. An innovation scorecard team was formed in the Czech Republic in 2019 in response to this request to complete a 3-year practical application project to measure the success of innovation in a typical project management environment.

The authors would like to thank Luděk Šmíd, Director Global Software Engineering, Red Hat in Brno, Czech Republic, for his support and contributions, direct and indirect, to this book. The same applies to the various operational teams within Red Hat we had the pleasure of working with over a 3-year period. Our sincere thanks for all their contributions and valuable insights.

Special thanks to the Association for Project Management (APM, UK) for publishing an initial article about our innovation scorecard concept in their *Project Magazine* during 2020.

Thanks go to SKEMA Business School in Lille, France (Prof Paul Gardiner), to allow us to present at their Eden annual international research conference to an audience of renowned and upcoming researchers.

Our sincere thanks go to the Project Management Institute (PMI) in the USA for publishing a series of short articles about our innovation scorecard during 2021.

And last, but not least, special thanks go to Springer Verlag in Germany for enabling us to publish our methodology.

About This Book

Our Vision

To establish and communicate the need to measure the success of innovation and changes across the industries, our methodology enables businesses and individuals to improve their skills in this area as a core competency, and to create a professional environment in which current and aspiring managers can consolidate and develop their innovation and change management skills.

Purpose and Scope of This Handbook

This handbook combines the accumulated experience of its authors with the best practice tools and techniques used in companies that already measure the success of innovation within their projects and other work environments. It provides a set of guidelines and procedures as a practical guide 'how to measure the success of innovation and change' in organisations. It is not a thesis on innovation management: there are many excellent training courses and books that can provide more detailed information on specific aspects of innovation management. Instead, it describes the general principles of how to measure the success of innovation or change, and then provides details of those procedures and processes that comprise the innovation scorecard methodology. This book will not present detailed discussions on how to introduce innovation within organisations—there are already lots of good publications available that cover this topic in detail. Any references to the concept of innovation (particularly Sect. 4.4) are purely intended to be supplementary to strengthen the presentation of the concept of our innovation scorecard.

The objectives of this handbook are:

- To improve the number, the quality, and the capability of people at work to conduct innovation measurements in projects/initiatives and other work environments.
- To help users implement a consistent approach to ensure that innovation measurement standards are maintained.

Table 1 Handbook structure

Part		
Part I	Introduction	Background information on the innovation scorecard concept.
	Glossary of Terms	Glossary of Terms used in this methodology
	Innovation Scorecard Design Process	Designing an innovation scorecard system for application at work. The innovation scorecard life cycle and gate process
	Tools and Techniques	Tools and techniques—common procedures and techniques to be used for effective management of the innovation scorecard through its life cycle
	References and Further Reading	
Part II	Case Study 1	A worked example of our first actual iScorecard case study (Atomic Host)
	Case Study 2	A worked example of our second actual iScorecard case study (Continuous Integration)
	Case Study 3	A worked example of our third iScorecard case study (Global Wi-Fi Roll-out)
Part III	Appendices	Supportive Documentation. Templates ready for use for any forthcoming innovation scorecard initiative/project

These guidelines provide the following additional benefits to users of our methodology:

- A useful and user-friendly guide of considered good practice to measure the success of innovations and change across a wide range of work environments including project management.
- A cohesive framework within which innovations and change management can be defined and controlled in a consistent manner.
- Clear definitions of the activities that need to be undertaken to be successful.
- Checklists to ensure that relevant areas should be covered at each stage of the stage gate approach.
- Standard procedures and templates ready for use by the community of practice.
- Guidelines on good innovation scorecard practice.
- Sharing the authors' suggested approach 'how to measure the success in innovations/change'.

The information contained within our pages is divided into three sections, as follows (Table 1).

Our publication brings together in a single volume all the essential information and guidance about the concept of innovation scorecard any potential user needs to know about so they can apply the content of this book immediately. In general, the authors have assumed that readers of this book have a working understanding of the associated concepts of change and project management. The intention is not to produce a prescriptive set of instructions that must be followed to the latter but rather a set of guidelines, which if followed intelligently, will increase the chances of innovations and changes being measured successfully.

Fig. 1 The iScorecard methodology summary diagram

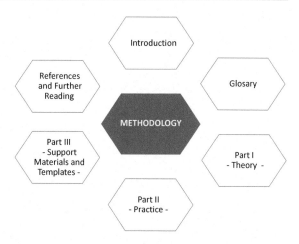

The templates and checklists provided should not be considered as restrictive or prescriptive. The authors have anticipated that work environments differ considerably. Users are encouraged to select from the appropriate techniques the most suitable for their specific needs and adapt to suit. Part I (Theory), in common with the methodology, is intended to support, not dictate, the implementation of our suggested innovation scorecard approach. Managers have considerable leeway in how to apply these within their work environments. There appears to be no better combination than a manager applying a well-structured methodology appropriately (Fig. 1).

Who Should Read This Handbook?

This title will be of interest to anyone who is involved in project and change management. Although it is primarily a reference guide in explaining how to manage the success of any innovation or change, it will also be useful:

- As a basis for the guidance and training of managers who are less experienced in managing innovations or change.
- As a source of potential background information for customers, suppliers, and contractors who need to understand more about the concept of an innovation scorecard.
- To set out to all those who sponsor, own, or contribute to innovation or change initiatives the innovation scorecard's approach to the realisation of business objectives.
- For change or innovation managers planning their career development.

Introduction

It appears that many companies across the industries are driven by ever-increasing demands to come up with new products and services to satisfy their customer needs and demands. To stay competitive, they need to respond positively and adopt new approaches on how to become and stay innovative in their outlook. Innovation management is not a new concept. It has been around since the 1960s. The value added by innovation has not always been measured regularly and consistently. Early concepts such as the so-called balanced scorecard developed by Kaplan and Norton (see Foreword) focused their attention primarily on business performance data. It was a strategic planning and management system that aligned daily work activities with strategy.

Today, the core question for any organisation is not whether 'to innovate or not' but 'how to innovate efficiently and effectively'. This drives the need to innovate wisely and with focus. It requires organisations to be capable of conducting continuous evaluations of their current innovation projects and of using this data to make decisions on whether to continue with their projects or not. Establishing effective forms of innovation efficiency measurement and management control as an information support for decision making undertaken at either the business or academic level is a very challenging task.

The authors adopted the following practical approach to apply an appropriate innovation scorecard concept for practical use and application within a primarily agile software development project in a Czech company. This included the utilisation of traditional techniques of 'measurement of returns' focusing on the cost control combined with strategic measurements over the long term together with financial objectives set by the project team. Selected relevant indicators were tailored to the organisation as each innovation is considered unique and specific. It is intended to bring competitive advantage to an organisation's growth. This approach resulted in a fit-for-purpose innovation scorecard methodology design that provides efficiency measurements and acts as a management control framework for innovations specific for, but not limited to, software development and IT industries, including other countries.

The detailed content may, at times, appear to be overwhelming. Readers can be rest assured that the presented 'wealth of data' is a necessary requirement to demonstrate the methodology's practical application value, irrespective of the industry it may be used within. The full presentation of 'what actually happened' aids in the full understanding of how to apply the methodology. It provides room for further thought how, for example, this methodology may need to be modified to consider the specific needs and requirements of individual organisations and the people who work within these. As the saying goes, one size does not fit all. This methodology acts as a good starting point for adopting an innovation scorecard measurement system that focuses on how successful changes and innovations have been.

The content of this handbook is of interest to both researchers and practitioners alike, irrespective of their level of experience in the field of measuring how success-ful innovations or changes have been. It is a practical guide which explains the various and different stages involved in setting up and managing an innovation scorecard system within organisations. All necessary details are explained simply and clearly and are presented in a logical sequence. New terms used are explained gradually so as not to bombard readers with jargon. Part I explains the theoretical nature of an innovation scorecard system and why this approach is considered an essential tool to measure how successful innovation or changes have been. Part II focuses on the practical application of the theoretical innovation scorecard frame-work. Three real-life case studies are presented in varying levels of detail to allow the reader to become familiar with, for example, the initial intricacies and challenges often associated with change management initiatives: Atomic Host, our first project, was a simple exploratory project to test our theories. We applied performance measurements after 'each round of activities (will be explained in more detail later), using just a few simple metrics to establish how successful, for example, any process changes have been (measured before and after the event). We were still learning, so we were 'walking' before 'running'. The second project, known as Continuous Integration (CI), was far more difficult and complex due to the inherent nature of this important part of software development. We applied three stages and three gates of the usual five stages and four gates model (Fig. 3.2). In addition, more metrics were developed to measure how successful any process changes have been (once again, measuring the results based on 'before' and 'after' performance data). Continuous Integration became our core project. And finally, we started our third project known as: Global Wi-Fi roll-out. This was our most difficult and largest project due to the scope and deliverables associated with this project. We added a fourth stage gate; the rest of the innovation scorecard principles and model remained similar when compared to our CI project. This was necessary so we could measure and manage the technical and engineering-driven work activities more effectively. The journey continues. . .

Contents

Part I

Theory

Applicability

1

Innovation Scorecard Practice Guidelines can be applied to any project irrespective of industry or geographical location, provided that local cultural differences are taken into consideration. This will ensure a consistent and coherent approach and application as intended by the authors. Project and business managers should consider the following prior to adopting the suggested approach in their projects and work environments:

- Specific projects or areas within projects that would benefit
- Business areas that would benefit from measuring the success of any innovation
- Meeting customer expectations, requirements, and needs (both internal and external)
- Considering any previous knowledge or experience of managing innovation
- Organisational readiness to measure how successful innovation in projects and work environments has been
- Necessity for additional resources
- Impact on current business, project management processes, methodology and training

To measure how successful any innovation has been, it is imperative that managers and project managers follow the guidelines suggested by this booklet and that they set themselves realistic and achievable performance measurements and targets. This includes regular target reviews.

Basic Requirements for an Innovation Scorecard System

2

This book is a guide to the process for developing, rolling out and the ongoing management of an Innovation Scorecard system that will assist both project and non-project managers to measure how successful innovation has been in their respective work areas.

The authors, who have over 60 years of theoretical and practical work experiences (between them) in areas of change management, suggest that an Innovation Scorecard can be applied across the industries and in any kind of company or organisation. It is important to note that local prevailing cultural differences need to be considered and appropriate adaptations will need to be made to make it fit its intended purpose irrespective of the work environment. The following list presents the fundamental high-level actions that need to be considered and completed before the Innovation Scorecard process can be started:

- Define the scope, including in and out of scope and the measurement background
- Develop a simple Work Breakdown Structure (WBS) to define the work that needs to be undertaken
- Develop stage-gate model
- Set performance objectives (WHAT) and Key Results (HOW)
- Define the measure characteristics
- Define calculations and data specifics
- Produce performance information
- Select innovation metrics
- Create an Innovation Scorecard Data Sheet

O. Zizlavsky, E. Fisher, *Innovation Scorecard*, Management for Professionals,
https://doi.org/10.1007/978-3-030-82688-8_2

What Is Meant by Innovation Scorecard?

3.1 Principles

First there was the concept of what is generally known as Balanced Scorecard. Over the years, a new theory emerged that took the original concept to new levels: Innovation Scorecard. Its focus was on innovation which also formed part of change management, and its strength lay in being a performance measurement and management control framework that had been developed to cope with 'all things innovation'. It appears that the two concepts of Balanced Scorecard and innovation fit together well for different reasons. Balanced Scorecard, on its own, is considered useful in areas where, for example, measured returns on innovation investment are not aligned with company strategy, where it is difficult to deploy appropriate financial indicators and where there is a lack of definition of strategy as far as the planning of innovation is concerned. Combining Balanced Scorecard with innovation brings distinct advantages that enable companies to cope with and manage better the accelerated scale of changes that have taken place recently across industries (Li & Dalton, 2003). According to Žižlavský (2016), the rate of growth in the size and scope of R&D departments has been spectacular and rapid, to the extent that problems of visibility are being generated. Managers feel that the basic decisions that were taken relatively easily years ago have now become extraordinarily difficult. In addition, Li and Dalton (2003) suggest that a lack of visibility from the top down develops serious problems that emerge from the bottom up. It is very difficult for people who work at an operational level to have a thorough understanding of the strategic vision of the company they work for.

In this context, it should be noted that the Czech business environment is idiosyncratic due to its prevailing cultural differences in terms of its modus operandi (Žižlavský, 2016). The developed Innovation Scorecard, specifically designed for this unique working environment, is based on 'the needs led' considerations by Kaplan and Norton (1996), the 'audit led' procedures considered by Dixon et al. (1990) and the 'consultant or facilitator led' approach suggested by Niven (2014). It is based on a Balanced Scorecard approach where balance is the equilibrium

© The Author(s), under exclusive license to Springer Nature Switzerland AG 2021
O. Zizlavsky, E. Fisher, *Innovation Scorecard*, Management for Professionals,
https://doi.org/10.1007/978-3-030-82688-8_3

between operative and strategic (short-term and long-term) goals, required inputs and outputs, internal and external performance indicators, and lagging/leading indicators. This includes financial and non-financial performance indicators. Each measurement is an inherent part of a chain of 'root cause and effect' links. According to Žižlavský (2016), most medium and large Czech companies, monitor performance of innovative activities by using specific financial and non-financial measures, but without any logical link between them. It appears that only a few companies, especially large ones, and those having different perspectives, understand the importance of the root cause-effect relationship between metrics, within this context. As a result, innovation evaluation proved to be most appropriate in favour of applying financial performance indicators.

The bringing together of the concepts of innovation and Balanced Scorecard all started with the outcomes of a primary research project that was supported by the Czech Scientific Foundation during 2013–2015. One of the main objectives of this research was to establish if organisations in the Czech Republic were measuring how effective and efficient innovations were. In addition, there was a desire to confirm what performance metrics were used, how these were applied and how effective these were. The outcome of this research confirmed that those companies who managed innovation effectively, were also obtaining valid and reliable innovation performance data, including evidence of the realised benefits arising from the application and management of innovation. When applied appropriately and in accordance with existing company strategy, marketing drives and HR/corporate policies, processes and procedures, innovation metrics provide managers and employees with opportunities to 'plan, organize, monitor and control' all innovation activities for the benefit of the organization they work for.

The next logical step was to implement the developed concept of Innovation Scorecard in practice to verify its suitability and functionality. This initiative resulted in the current project called "Innovation Scorecard: A Management Control Framework for an Innovation Project within the IT/Software Development industry", supported by the Technology Agency of the Czech Republic. The duration of the project is 3 years during which best current practices in the IT/Software Development industry will be identified. Several associated theories and practice-based case studies were:

- Designed
- Tested
- Developed
- Rolled out (in an operational work environment)

3.2 Benefits

Putting theory into practice in a fast-moving software development competitive environment in the Czech Republic proved to be a real challenge that was worth following up on. To overcome the usual scepticism and suspicion associated with the introduction of changes how people work and perform at work, our team took the conscious decision to be authentic and genuine right from the word 'go' with all involved parties. Collaboration and consultation were key approaches. Some pushes from our side were necessary to instill in key stakeholders the value of deploying an Innovation Scorecard system within Red Hat, Czech Republic. This organisation is a research and development subsidiary of Red Hat, settled in Brno. It was formed in 2006 and has around 1300 employees. It is a private limited company that operates in the software industry. The parent company, Red Hat, founded in 1993 and headquartered in Raleigh, North Carolina, chose to set up this subsidiary in the Czech Republic in favour of other locations due to the Czech Republic's position to increase the awareness and improve the perception of open-source software advocacy. The application of our suggested Innovation Scorecard process (Fig. 3.1) is not limited to IT or software development projects or initiatives. Subject to taking prevailing local cultural differences into account and modifying the process 'as required', it is considered fit for purpose for use across the industries project managers operate within.

We considered that Red Hat was an ideal candidate for our project. They appeared to have a high innovation potential considered a suitable characteristic of the company's existing innovation environment (to create, develop and implement something new). It is an essential feature that includes change, development, learning, flexibility, creativity and the ability or tendency to adapt.

The Innovation Scorecard team focused their attention on the doing rather than the talking to ensure that Red Hat achieved maximum return on their Innovation Scorecard investment. The team had to ensure that a high performing innovator like Red Hat accepted that the team applied the usual project management skills (plan, organise, monitor and control) to the full life cycle of the Innovation Scorecard process. Not an easy task when working in an Agile/SCRUM sprint-based work environment where doing is of paramount importance and planning appears to be taking a secondary position!

The team developed three smaller sub-projects deemed most appropriate for the start of this initiative: Atomic Host (completed in 2019), Continuous Integration (completed in 2020) and Global Wi-Fi (ongoing, 2021). The 'working' details for all these projects are presented in Part B (Case Studies).

The aim was to keep the change momentum going so that Red Hat could ultimately implement and maintain some leading-edge innovative work approaches over a longer period once the initial innovation projects had been completed. The main and overall Innovation Scorecard project commenced at the beginning of 2019 and will finish by the end of 2021.

3.3 Measuring Success—Theory

As mentioned before, the adopted Innovation Scorecard concept is a conceptual project management control framework specifically designed for working environments that thrive on innovation and/or change management, especially

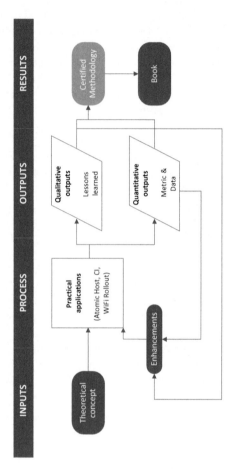

Fig. 3.1 Innovation Scorecard rollout process in Red Hat

Table 3.1 Innovation Scorecard theoretical background

Method	What (Author)
Balanced Scorecard	Balance between financial/non-financial metrics, short/long-term goals (Kaplan & Norton, 1996) Sequence 'Aim–Cause and Effect–Metric–Target Value' (Horváth, 2011) Scorecard design (Niven, 2014) Number of metrics (Kaplan & Norton, 1996) Casual links—strategy maps (Cokins, 2009) Balanced Scorecard and innovation (Gama et al., 2007; Garcia-Valderrama et al., 2008)
Innovation management	Innovation pipeline (such as Bessant & Tidd, 2011; Davila et al., 2013) Input–Process–Output–Outcome Model (ISO, 2021) Stage Gate Model (Cooper, 2008) Open innovation (Chesbrough, 2003)
Project management	Wingate (2015), APM Body of Knowledge (2019)
Scorecard data sheet design	Niven (2014), Parmenter (2015)
Performance measurement systems design	Bourne et al. (2003), Horvath (2011), Kaplan and Norton (1996)

within the IT and Software Development industries in the Czech Republic. This research's primary objective was to ascertain whether organisations in the Czech Republic measure the efficiency of their innovations and what metrics they applied to measure these. Results confirmed that organisations who constantly managed innovation were engaged in identifying performance measurements to determine the level of value and benefits associated with innovation. When applied appropriately and in accordance with existing company strategy, marketing drives and HR/corporate policies, processes and procedures, innovation metrics provide managers and employees with opportunities to plan, to organise, to manage and to control all innovation activities for the benefit of the organization they work for. The Innovation Scorecard was proposed as a solution to support these activities and to create the basis for improved business decision making. It aligns and integrates popular innovation management and management control approaches (Table 3.1).

It is based on a Balanced Scorecard approach where balance is an equilibrium between operative and strategic (short-term and long-term) goals, required inputs and outputs, internal and external performance criteria, and lagging/leading indicators. This includes the financial and non-financial performance indicators. Each measurement is an inherent part of a chain of 'root cause-and-effect' links.

The theoretical background, structure (including processes) and methodology of the suggested Innovation Scorecard can be divided into distinct stages including some management decision gates to aid control. The suggested Innovation Scorecard approach incorporates the core functions of leading innovative teams such as to define tasks, plan, control, evaluate and support. This effective and efficient approach to introduce the concept of Innovation Scorecard into an organization is vital for moving innovations from the idea to launch phase in a systematic and managed way. The proposed Innovation Scorecard (Fig. 3.2) suggests six distinct

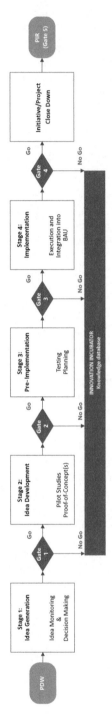

Fig. 3.2 Applied Innovation Scorecard process

stages controlled by gates where Go/No Go decisions are made whether to proceed to the next gate: Gate 1 Idea Generation; Gate 2 Idea Development (including pilot studies/testing); Gate 3 Pre-implementation planning; Gate 4 Implementation (Roll-out or Going Live); Gate 5 Closed Down (Post Implementation Review including Lessons Learned/Knowledge Management).

Such a stage gate system is designed to work as a 'funnel' that begins with 'screening the ideas or projects/initiatives' during the early stages when fewer resources are utilised and continues throughout the life of the project/initiative. An innovation (project) leader is in charge in each stage to ensure that the innovation project/initiative meets all the required criteria to pass the gate and moves forward to the next stage. The stage gate system can also improve the effectiveness and productivity in the execution of key project/initiative tasks. It provides a framework to control whether, for example, a project/initiative should be discontinued. For example, a project/initiative may look quite promising at the outset but may have to be 'culled' during later stages if it turns out to be no longer viable to be completed. Equally, 'culled' projects/initiatives can be 'revived' later when, for example, there has been a change in business needs. We suggest considering a so-called 'innovation incubator' process to aid this decision-making (Fig. 3.2). It is vital that unviable and unsuitable projects/initiatives are stopped immediately if they are not right for the organization for justified reasons. This stops unnecessary resources from being engaged on aborted work that could be better employed elsewhere (Lindegaard, 2015).

3.4   Measuring Success—Practice

From a managerial viewpoint, the Innovation Scorecard may provide useful guidelines for focusing attention and expending resources during the entire innovation process. It is argued that the informed use of evaluation metrics as guideposts for increased managerial attention and the identification of problems may help management to prevent drop-and-go-errors in their innovation efforts.

We considered that the implementation of the Innovation Scorecard would contribute to improving the efficiency, ways of working, economies of scale (operational level) and the ultimate competitiveness of Red Hat in different ways:

- Improved informed decision making by empowering staff more (staff becoming more independent)
- A significant reduction in software development rework time due to agile and innovative process improvements (having a positive effect on the company's Return on Investment (ROI)
- Time savings can be used to deploy the same staff on other tasks thus improving operational efficiency by being able to deliver more in less time to the same or higher quality parameters (higher productivity)

- An increase in dynamic response approaches in relation to business changes due to attitudinal changes in staff driven by innovative idea generation and process improvements (staff viewing changes as something positive)

In summary, the researchers consider that the following benefit realizations can be achieved through the roll-out and implementation of an Innovation Scorecard concept within Red Hat (our pilot study was limited to work process changes/ innovations within this work area. Other potential work areas such as Human Resources, Marketing or Research & Development were out of scope in the context of our research. This also placed a limitation on our developed performance measurement metrics (Sect. 4.6):

- Higher profitability through the overall value of innovation from a market and product perspective
- Maximize Return on Investment (ROI)
- Higher staff productivity levels through business change including improved organisational alignment and 'ways of working' (modus operandi)
- Improved streamlining of software development processes through the roll-out of an Innovation Scorecard System across different associated projects
- Improved timely Communication (internal and external)

3.5   The Four Pillars of an Innovation Scorecard

We suggest following and applying these four 'work behaviours' to ensure that any innovation initiative is managed effectively right from the start. These are not in any order of priority or importance:

Plan
Conduct a simple 'brain storming' session, either by yourself or together with team members, to capture what it is you are trying to achieve. Do not be too specific. High level details are fine. Anything goes at this stage. Listen well to what others have to say and include your own views, too. Be open-minded and welcome inputs no matter how 'bizarre' they may seem at the time. Create headings so you can group together activities by topic such as work practices, communication standards and team productivity that you wish to measure/improve.

Organise
The next step is to go through these topics either on your own or in a team environment to create a logical order for each heading and to delete any irrelevant or unnecessary activity. When this has been completed, conduct a final check (preferably with inputs from the team) before you can start implementing the desired innovation/change project/initiative.

Monitor and Control

Now that 'planning' has been completed, the next two steps are concerned with making sure that things are getting done (own work and that of others) and that the innovation project/initiative is controlled by a single owner: You! (Sect. 5.3). Keeping an eye on progress made is vital to ensuring the successful completion of the project/initiative. This can be a complex and dauting task, depending on how many people are involved in the innovation. You should consider the following approaches to keep up to date with what goes on in your innovation project/initiative and to stay in control of the delivery of major milestones:

- Regular face to face communications with core team members (formal and informal)
- Video and Conference Calls
- E-mails and setting up a Shared Drive (for ease of access to relevant information by those who need to have access to this information)
- Weekly/Monthly Progress Reports
- Stage Gate Reviews
- Scheduling

References

Association for Project Management. (2019). *Body of knowledge* (7th ed.). Association for Project Management (APM).

Bessant, J., & Tidd, J. (2011). *Innovation and entrepreneurship*. Wiley.

Bourne, M. C. S., Neely, A. D., Mills, J. F., & Platts, K. W. (2003). Implementing performance measurement systems: A literature review. *International Journal of Business Performance Management, 5*(1), 1–24.

Chesbrough, H. (2003). *Open innovation: The new imperative for creating and profiting from technology*. Harvard Business School.

Cokins, G. (2009). *Performance management: Integrating strategy execution, methodologies, risk, and analytics*. Wiley.

Cooper, R. G. (2008). Perspective: The Stage-Gate idea-to-launch process – update, What's new and NextGenSystems. *Journal of Product Innovation Management, 25*, 213–232.

Davila, T., Epstein, M. J., & Shelton, R. D. (2013). *Making innovation work: How to manage it, measure it, and profit from it*. FT Press.

Dixon, J. R., Nanni, A. J., & Vollmann, T. E. (1990). *The new performance challenge: Measuring operations for world-class competition*. Irwin Professional Pub.

Gama, N. J., Da Silva, M. M., & Ataide, J. (2007). A Balanced Scorecard: A Balanced Scorecard for measuring the value added by innovation. In *Digital enterprise technology: Perspectives and future challenges*. Springer.

García-Valderrama, T., Mulero-Mendigorri, E., & Revuelta-Bordoy, D. (2008). A Balanced Score-card framework for R&D. *European Journal of Innovation Management, 11*(2), 241–281.

Horváth, P. (2011). *Controlling*. Vahlen.

International Standards Organisation (ISO). (2021). [on-line]. Accessed June 10, 2021, from https://www.iso.org

Kaplan, R. S., & Norton, D. P. (1996). *The Balanced Scorecard: Translating strategy into action*. Harvard Business School Press.

Li, G., & Dalton, D. (2003). Balanced Scorecard for I+D. *Pharmaceutical Executive, 23*(3), 84–90.

Lindegaard, S. (2015). *The execution of innovation: What you need to know* [on-line]. http://i. hypeinnovation.com/execution-white-paper-0

Niven, P. R. (2014). *Balanced Scorecard evolution: A dynamic approach to strategy execution*. Wiley.

Parmenter, D. (2015). *Key performance indicators: Developing, implementing, and using winning KPIs*. Wiley.

Wingate, L. M. (2015). *Project management for research and development: Guiding innovation for positive R&D outcomes*. CRC Press.

Žižlavský, O. (2016). *Innovation Scorecard: Conceptual performance measurement and management framework for innovation process*. Vutium Press.

Innovation Scorecard Design Process

4

Efficient and complex measurement systems are essential and crucial to the success of innovations. It is not enough just to pick a few areas, use random indicators and expect to obtain the information needed for managing innovations. It ends up mostly in a situation where the competent managers are overwhelmed with analysis results that they do not use in their work or that they use in a completely inefficient manner. This approach is time consuming and draining on productivity. It can also lead to inconsistent analyses and incorrect measures. A fundamental rule of innovation management says: "*Linking strategy to innovation measurement with a few sharp metrics provides a clear picture of performance.*" (Davilla et al., 2013, p. 146).

The following innovation performance measurement rules were compiled based on best practice in companies such as GE, Apple, Toyota and 3M.

- What gets measured gets done, so be careful what you measure.
- Understand the strategy and business model of innovation for your organisation and build a measurement system for innovation that is tied to both.
- Know what you want to achieve with each measurement system at each organisational level of the company. There are three options: communicate the strategy and the underlying mental models, monitor performance, and learn.
- Tailor the innovation measurement system to match the mix of incremental, semi radical, and radical innovation strategies.
- Change your measurements as your strategy and company change.
- Build your innovation performance measurement system to avoid barriers to its success (Davilla et al., 2013).

It is for these reasons that the design of an Innovation Scorecard must be conducted in an orderly structured and logical sequence. A strictly followed approach provides the foundation for an effective approach to measure the success of any innovation in work environments. When measuring innovation, measurements usually depend on two conditions: efficiency and economy. It appears that both need to be applied together so that the measurement of innovation can be

O. Zizlavsky, E. Fisher, *Innovation Scorecard*, Management for Professionals, https://doi.org/10.1007/978-3-030-82688-8_4

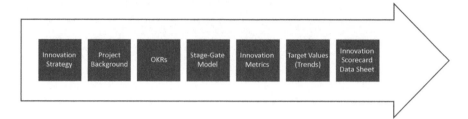

Fig. 4.1 Innovation Scorecard design process

completed with a higher level of success. When used on their own, each does not attract sufficient attention for this to work well. It is therefore important that a comprehensive system with several indicators is used to assess the capabilities and success of any innovation. Multiple indicators can examine the innovation process from several angles or approaches, thus displaying a comprehensive and 'actual picture of the process'. Our suggested basic structure of the Innovation Scorecard Design process includes the stages shown in Fig. 4.1.

This section comprises descriptions and specifications of tools and techniques to support the management of any innovation in typically agile work environments but is not limited to these. It is our paradigm that our Innovation Scorecard approach can be applied in any kind of working environment, including projects and so-called 'Business as Usual' (BAU). The templates and checklist examples we provide should not be considered as restrictive or prescriptive. It is accepted that innovations vary in nature considerably. Users of our methodology need to select from the appropriate techniques for their project and adapt to suit. We suggest that certain topics, for example, innovation strategy, objectives and key results, metrics (Fig. 4.1), are mandatory in form and ally very closely to rigorous stages in the suggested innovation life cycle. We consider these to be essential elements of the whole process. In addition, and based on the general principles of project management, some techniques such as risk management and producing a so-called work breakdown structure, are advisory. The user of our suggested Innovation Scorecard methodology has considerable leeway in how to apply these at work as they wish and deem necessary. Further details of these and any other considered relevant tools and techniques will be discussed and presented. This section, in common with the methodology, is intended to support, not dictate, the implementation of measuring the success of innovation at work in any work environment across the many industries. There is no better combination than a good change manager applying a well-constructed methodology appropriately.

We have produced a list of what we consider are the key essential activities that apply to this section (Table 4.1).

Table 4.1 Considered key activities: Innovation Scorecard

Activity/comment	Section/chapter
Defining Innovation Strategy	4.1
Presenting the Background	4.2
Developing Objectives and Key Results (OKRs)	4.3
Designing the Stage Gate Model	4.4
Innovation Metrics	4.5
Innovation Scorecard Data Sheet	4.6
Tools and Techniques	5

4.1   Defining Innovation Strategy

We suggest that the strategy formulation must precede any process, including innovation itself. Therefore, the core presumptions for the Innovation Scorecard Design process are that the organisation has defined its innovation strategy and its innovation business model. This means the organisation had defined the framework in which it will operate and according to which it will select its innovation initiative. Strategy depends on the resources of the company, and it should take the external market forces of the company such as competitors and customers into account (Tidd et al., 2005). An innovation strategy needs clear strategic leadership and direction plus optimum allocation of resources to make it happen. The formulation and definition of what is meant by innovation strategy is a task that needs to be owned by senior management of the organisation. We suggest that this needs to be a 'top down' approach. Setting the direction of the company, defining the corporate goals, and describing the corporate vision, must not be delegated. Each organisation needs to define its innovation strategy. There is no list of available strategies to 'pick and choose' from. This difficult high-level strategic thinking needs to be conducted as a matter of priority before any serious work is started. Every organisation must develop their own innovation strategy, be prepared to adapt to changing conditions, and then choose the right time to implement the planned changes.

Vital strategic questions must be answered including the following (in no order or priority):

- What does the company want to achieve? How does the innovation portfolio need to be shaped in the future in relation to products, regions, and customers? In which business fields does the company intend to operate?
- How does the company wish to manage competition? What are the most important core competencies to form long-term success?
- How does the company intend to achieve its intended positioning within the market it operates in?
- What are the necessary actions the business needs to consider if it wishes to expand, restructure, or downsize? What are the potential implications for its growth strategy? (Thomaschewski & Tarlatt, 2010, p. 129).

- Will any considered innovation help to reach the company's strategic goals, for example, to achieve set targets in terms of growth, market share or increasing the profit margin?
- Does the business understand why there is a need to innovate? Does the business have sufficient knowledge to manage the planned innovation? Is the business ready for change? Does the business understand how to obtain the desired knowledge if this is not readily available internally? (Bessant & Tidd, 2011, p. 552).
- Is the planned innovation unique and is it aligned to the business vision?
- How does the innovation fit in with what the business's competitors are engaged in? Is there a potential threat to the business from traditional and non-traditional competitors?
- Will the innovation stretch the company in terms of challenges and limitations?
- Will it foster passion among current and future management and company leadership?
- Is the company ready to take on board innovation in terms of budget, effort required and making the best use of their people?
- Does the approach provide targets for experimentation and learning?
- Will the company be united in their thinking and actions 'what to do and what not to do?
- Will the company be able to act consistently and achieve cumulative results within set time scales? (Skarzynski & Gibson, 2008, p. 155).

We suggest that a full-time change manager should be appointed if the innovation initiative stretches across functions within the organisation, particularly if the innovation is complex and carries a high profile. Normal practice is to ask line mangers to manage any innovation, provided their suitability for this task has been assessed adequately through a competency assessment, for example. It is also possible to train less experienced managers to take on board this important role-they may need some help and support from more experienced colleagues. The effective management of innovation required a team effort. Whilst it is essential to have clear roles and responsibilities for each change management team member, the innovation initiative will only succeed if there is a mutually supportive partnership. Not only is each change initiative unique but also the management approach and management style requirements change during the life cycle.

The formulation of a clear strategy, integration of employees, comprehensible and consistent communication and flexibility seem to be the main prerequisites for an effective innovation process and at least for a rapid commercialisation of new ideas. These factors are not only important for the innovation, but also are prerequisites for change management such as the APMBok, 2019, Sect. 1.1.3. The management of an innovation process and the management of a change process are intertwined as the innovation process involves constant adaptation as well as the way people cope with each other in this process. Companies therefore need people who are empowered and enabled to drive change and innovation. This will only be successful provided that any deviances from any planned work are monitored effectively and appropriate corrective actions can be taken to put things right. Therefore, an evaluation of the change and innovation processes is vital. Only a continuous, holistic evaluation enables the planned and actual situation to be compared to adapt, if necessary. And this adaptation, again, is the task of a successful farsighted management.

Section 4.2 presents some considered 'background actions' that need to be carried out to get any innovation initiative 'up and running'. This list is not finite nor are the actions in any order of priority. Users of the methodology are encouraged to add their own actions to this list as they think necessary.

4.2 Presenting the Background

When initiating the concept of an Innovation Scorecard for a specific work area or project, it is important that all parties involved agree in considerable detail why this initiative or project is important and what it is expected to achieve. We suggest that the owner of the initiative produces a simple but effective document that captures all the necessary high-level details whilst acting as a kind of 'tick list' for the owner to ensure that all the identified activities will be completed and delivered in a timely manner. This document can be used in both project and non-project work environments but is referred to here as a project definition document or PDD. It needs to be produced at the beginning of a change or innovation initiative to ensure that all important aspects of the planned and considered work have been captured well in a single location. We recommend that the document owner applies a simple but effective project management approach based on the so-called 'BOSCARD' principle (Table 4.2). The acronym stands for background, objectives, scope, constraints, assumptions, risks, and deliverables. This document needs to be reviewed regularly and updated by the document owner as and when important or significant changes have occurred. The document provides a sound basis for effective management progress reporting and decision-making.

In addition to the PDD, other typical project management tools and techniques can be used. We present a list and details of the ones we consider most relevant and important in Chap. 5. We also consider that the following activities need to be put in place at the beginning of an Innovation Scorecard initiative to control its progress (add your own as our list is not exhaustive):

- Initiate weekly phone calls (or face to face where possible) with those involved in the initiative to check progress and assess what needs to be done during the next reporting period.
- Set up a simple spreadsheet and call it something like 'Project Action List'. This document contains details of the work in progress and the work that has been completed. This includes the start date, the task owner, any details of the work, and when it was completed (Appendix A). We suggest that the owner of the initiative sets up a so-called traffic light system (Red, Amber and Green or RAG) to show the status of each action (red means there are significant issues with the

Table 4.2 BOSCARD structure (https://www.projectsmart.co.uk/boscard.php)

Background	Provide background information that includes the reasons why the project is considered necessary and what the project is expected to deliver, how and by when. Include the reasons why an Innovation Scorecard approach has been adopted to measure the success of any innovation/change.
Objectives	Describe the Innovation Scorecard initiative objectives-focus on what the Innovation Scorecard needs to achieve, such as process improvements.
Scope	Provide clear and unambiguous details of what the Innovation Scorecard initiative will focus on, what it will do. Include details of what is within and what is out of scope.
Constraints	Identify any specific constraints or restrictions that limit or place conditions on the initiative, especially those associated with its scope. Constraints can include elements of time, cost, quality, or specification.
Assumptions	Specify what has been assumed for the application of the Innovation Scorecard in the absence of certain knowledge. Assumptions need to be agreed with those who have a vested interest in the change initiative.
Risks	Carry out a risk assessment (high, medium, or low) for the change initiative. Just focus on what may or may not happen that could potentially stop the initiative or have a serious impact on its planned delivery. Focus on Innovation Scorecard application risks.
Deliverables	State clearly what the initiative will deliver. This can be based on the objectives identified earlier. The main must be on yielding, for example, process improvements, and achieving major milestones identified for the effective application of the Innovation Scorecard.

resolution and this requires urgent attention including escalation to senior management), amber means that there are some minor issues but these are dealt with by the owner, and green means that the action has been completed in a timely manner/all is well).

- Record and summarise what has been discussed during formal initiative review meetings, with your primary focus being on the Innovation Scorecard elements. Capture all action points arising from the meeting and transfer these to the 'project action list' introduced above. This will put you in control of the actions. Monitor the completion of all outstanding actions regularly and take appropriate action where necessary to move their completion to a satisfactory conclusion.

4.3   Developing Objectives and Key Results (OKRs)

Section 4.2 presented our suggestion to produce a Project Definition Document (PDD) right at the start of any innovation initiative. An important part of this document is to develop the key objectives of the initiative. This needs to include details of what the objectives are expected to achieve, how these will be achieved and who will 'own' the objectives. Clear ownership of the objectives is vital to ensure there are no 'grey areas' ('But I thought you were responsible for this objective'…). We suggest that the owner of the initiative needs to do some high-level strategic thinking first to develop the objectives, considering, for example, what it is the innovation initiative is trying to achieve. Once the potential list of objectives has been completed, the owner needs to review this list and put all objectives in order of their priority, and then select the most relevant objectives. The number of objectives must be commensurate with the desired outcomes of the initiative. All considered objectives must be aligned with the overall innovation strategy (Sect. 4.1).

Organisation innovation initiatives achieve very little when objectives are too vague, concept of supply and demand have not been taken into consideration and associated performance metrics have not been clearly defined or are missing (Sect. 4.3). Innovation leaders must set explicit targets based on innovation metrics, and gain commitment from senior management to achieve them. Innovation leaders need to consider that metrics are part of a broader system and that they must reflect the unique culture of the company as well as the competitive realities in the markets they operate within. The quality of the objectives is a major criterion for the successful implementation of an Innovation Scorecard system. It has a significant influence on its successful launch and implementation. Poorly defined objectives can adversely affect the successful implementation of such as system. We recommend you consider the following suggestions when setting your objectives:

- Each initiative should not contain more than four or five objectives-focus on clarity.
- Describe each objective by using active verbs and use single sentences.
- Focus on the innovation goals that carry the greatest strategic significance for the business in terms of competitive advantage.
- Ensure that all objectives are specific-avoid ambiguity.
- Think creatively and do not worry at this point about how 'measurable' objectives are.

Processing and documenting the relationships between cause and effect among individual innovation objectives is one of the key elements of any Innovation Scorecard system. There is a relationship between cause and effect as far as innovative considerations are concerned. We suggest that innovation objectives are not separate and independent but are connected and influence each other. The success of an innovation strategy is thus dependent on the collective action of various factors that include, for example, so-called critical success factors (CSF). In this context, it is essential that appropriate and relevant CSFs are designed and developed for each objective to ensure that the innovation leader achieves the set targets by concentrating on what is most important and 'critical' to achieve this. In addition, we suggest that key results should be considered. They are subordinate to CSFs and support the achievement of objectives (see a working example at Table 4.3 below). Key results measure the quantitative results of business actions. They can help to measure quantitative results (for example, how many times something has happened) and to achieve the set objectives.

Table 4.3 OKRs example (Doerr, 2018)

Example 1—Intel story	Example 2—Intuit story
Objective	**Objective**
Demonstrate the 8080s superior performance (=WHAT) as compared to the Motorola 6800 (=HOW)	Modernise, rationalise, and secure the technology to run the business of Intuit
Key Results	**Key Results**
(As measured by...)	(As measured by...)
1. Deliver five 'benchmarks'	1. Complete the migration of the Oracle
2. Develop a 'demonstration'	eBusiness Suite to R12 and entire 11.5.9. This
3. Develop sales training materials for the	quarter
'field force'	2. Deliver wholesale billing as a platform
4. Call on three customers to prove the system	capability by the end of the FY16
works	3. Complete onboarding of 'agents' from the
	small business unit into the sales force team

4.4 Innovation Scorecard Life Cycle

A typical innovation process can be divided into distinct stages and should be separated by management decision gates. This is generally referred to as a 'life cycle'. We have adopted this project management concept for our Innovation Scorecard system and developed a sequence of 'stages' and 'gates' to fit our purpose. However, one size does not fit the requirements of all innovation leaders. We suggest that innovation leaders use our generic life cycle suggestion as a starting point for their initiatives and modify or delete stages and gates to meet their requirements. This section provides full details of each stage and gate of our adopted life cycle approach, including the main activities associated with each stage and any procedures for stage-specific tasks.

Our adopted Innovation Scorecard life cycle (Fig. 3.2, Sect. 3.3) has the following standard stage and gate sequence we applied in our three case studies in Red Hat, Brno, Czech Republic (Part II: Case Studies 1, 2 and 3). Although the life cycle was specific for software development process improvements, it can be adapted to fit any kind of innovation initiative. For example, not all stages or gates may be required for your specific needs. A system that is fast and flexible at the same time and a system that can respond to changes swiftly adds value to users of an agile approach. Focusing on results rather than adhering to a rigid and strict process is of paramount importance to the successful delivery of so-called 'agile' projects or work. We suggest designing a unique stage-gate model for each project/initiative according to its specific needs and in line with its characteristics. The number of gates can be radically reduced (Case Study 1), the approach can be 'lean' (for example, we used only three gates in Case Study 2), or it can be used cumulatively (Case Study 3).

It is therefore essential to conduct your thinking first what it is you are trying to improve and measure, and then design and develop a life cycle that suits. You can rename your stages by giving them meaningful titles that make it clear what each stage will 'cover' or deliver:

- Stage 1: Idea Generation
- Stage 2: Idea Development
- Stage 3: Pre-implementation Planning
- Stage 4: Implementation and integration into Business as Usual (BAU, use after lifespan)
- Stage 5: Post Implementation Review

The purpose of a gate is to describe the procedures/actions that are associated with each stage. These need to be completed before you can proceed to the next stage. A gate is a kind of 'enabler' to move forward to the next stage, provided all activities/actions have been completed successfully. The primary objective of a stage is to validate requirements and ensure that, for example, the innovation leader is authorised to progress the initiative. Let us now take a closer look at each gate of our suggested life cycle and the details that are associated with these. Appendix C (Case Studies: Atomic Host and Continuous Integration) provides detailed practical application details for Stages 1–5).

4.4.1 Measuring the Inventive Phase (Gate 1 and 2)

Gate 1 Idea Generation
Every innovation starts with an idea or concept and finishes when the idea has been completed – typically, with the launch of a new product, service, or process. This means an effective as well as an efficient approach, so that the innovation can be moved from idea to launch in a systematic way. Every stage is preceded by one gate. At each stage information is gathered to reduce project uncertainties and risks which is then evaluated at the gate that follows. Gates represent decision points with deliverables (what the innovation team brings to the decision point) and must-meet/should-meet criteria where you need to decide if you wish to proceed with the innovation project/initiative or if it is to be stopped, temporarily paused or 'culled'. Gates are sometimes referred to as "Go/No-Go check points" where a decision to invest more or not is made (Cooper, 2008). Any gate that does not meet the 'proceed criteria' should be stopped and resources should be allocated to other promising initiatives. Figure 3.2 presents a typical 'starter' stage-gate model for the Innovation Scorecard concept.

Gate 1 focuses on developing and designing new ideas how to measure innovation in projects/initiatives or how to introduce innovation into existing work areas. This phase enables you to capture new as well as existing ideas, irrespective whether these originate internally or externally to the organisation. 'Idea screening' starts when all ideas have been collected. It is the first in a series of evaluations that focus on whether any considered ideas fit in with the organisation's strategy. It acts as a kind of 'filtering' system to separate valid ideas from impractical ones. Any ideas that pass this stage can then move on to Stage 2. This principle applies to any further adopted stages.

We have prepared an 'idea question sample checklist' that you can use to generate some initial ideas where to measure the success of any innovation or where you wish to improve/innovate, for example, current work processes. This list is intended to get you started on the road to identify where in your business the Innovation Scorecard could be applied. This list is not exhaustive nor is it in any order of priority:

- How radical is the idea?
- How big or how important could it be?
- What immediate or short-range gains or results can be anticipated?
- How simple or complex will the idea's execution or implementation be?
- Could you work out several variations of the idea? Could you offer alternative views?
- How soon could the idea be put into operation?
- Will the idea encourage the measurement of how successful a new product/ service/process has been?

> Note: We suggest not to ask questions that relate to profitability during the 'idea generation stage' so you do not get side-tracked by financial implications. Focus should be on the actual generation of ideas.

Typical areas where it is possible to measure how successful the delivery of, for example, set goals has been achieved, could include topics such as staff churn rate (employee turnover), how many applicants applied for an advertised position (effectiveness of the recruitment process) or how many employees in the company engaged actively in the 'staff suggestion scheme'. These so-called 'goal measures' need to be designed and developed carefully. They need to fit in with business strategy and objectives and operational needs.

We recommend producing a high-level draft Project Definition Document (PDD, Appendix B) at this stage but only for viable and potential ideas that have a good chance of being selected for progressing to the next stage. It is not essential (nice to have), but it should be given consideration by the initiative owner.

The focus should also be on measuring how responsive the company is to needs for business change/innovation and its 'readiness for change' state. This includes a sanity check whether the business has devoted sufficient resources to undertake change/innovation activities cross-functionally in the following areas:

- Talent Management
- Financial Commitment
- Knowledge Management
- Quality Management
- Communication Management
- Pre and Post Implementation Surveys

Table 4.4 Gate 1 checklist

Stage 1 checklist

Category	Deliverable/activity	Owner	Tick if complete
Compulsory	Identify areas of the business in need for change or improvement	Head of Department	
Essential	Prepare an Idea Generation Proposal (high level)	Initiative Owner	
Essential	Conduct competitor analysis	Initiative Owner	
Nice to have	Prepare (high level) budget and resource requirements	Initiative Owner	
Nice to have	High level draft Project Definition Document (PDD)	Initiative Owner	

Table 4.4 below shows a suggested typical Concept Stage checklist. You can change this template to suit your individual needs.

Gate 2 Idea Development (Proof-of-concept)
This section describes the steps associated with developing ideas from Gate 1 further. These are not in any order of priority. Its purpose is to:

- Review and evaluate ideas that were generated in Stage 1
- Select only the most feasible ideas to proceed
- Confirm that the selected ideas will work
- Prepare a preliminary list of deliverables for each chosen idea
- Develop the 'proof of concept' for the final ideas
- Conduct testing
- Prepare a resource estimate for the chosen ideas (high-level)
- Prepare a risk assessment for the completion of the selected ideas
- Prepare a 'To do list' for the involved team
- Update the Project Definition Document (PDD)
- Plan for next stage

Before we delve into providing some details 'how to manage the above points', we suggest planning and organising all the considered activities that will be necessary to measure the success of a change or innovation. Grouping together all your initial thoughts under the above headings is a good starting point. It enables you to gather all the right information so you can make an informed decision. This is never an easy task. You should consider all cross-functional impacts including any potential dependencies where work must be completed sequentially such as 'Activity A needs to be completed fully before Activity B can start'.

One of the first tasks associated with Gate 2 is to review and evaluate the ideas you generated in Gate 1. Check each idea for suitability and viability and ensure that it fits in with business and/or operational needs. Give ideas that carry some strategic importance additional 'weighting' during your assessment. We suggest using a scale 'Out of 10' for this initial analysis. Consider whether it is possible to implement the considered ideas ('Will this work in our business'?).

Be radical in your approach when making the final choice. Select the most viable ideas and do not get side-tracked by any 'nice to have' thoughts. Focus your attention on what is most important and in the best interest of the organization. Where necessary, conduct a final 'sanity check' that your selected ideas are a strategic fit.

Develop and prepare a preliminary list of all considered work activities (deliverables that you need to undertake to achieve the completion of each selected idea. A simple spreadsheet is sufficient (see Appendix A). In addition, we suggest that you complete a 'To Do' list where you list the outstanding tasks of those involved in the initiative, including date, name, details of the work to be done, comments and the completion date.

We recommend applying a 'proof of concept' approach during Gate 2 to determine whether considered ideas can be turned into reality. For example, it would show whether the idea could be 'rolled out', in business operations, from a management point of view.

Complete a sufficiently detailed resource estimate for the completion of each idea. This should include hours of effort for each task plus required tools and any training needs. It provides an overview of the potential costs associated with each idea and aids to decide whether to proceed with the idea or not.

We suggest conducting a risk assessment for each idea, using high, medium, and low classification criteria. Consider the likelihood and probability of something happening and assess the impact this could have on your idea roll-out. It is advisable to think about how to mitigate each risk should it materialise (what we will do if this happens). Spending a little bit of thinking time to explore potential solutions is a good investment.

The initiative owner needs to update the Project Definition Document (PDD) and incorporate any changes/additions that have been adopted during this this stage. Keeping this document up to date is of paramount importance.

He/she should make time to focus on what needs to be done in the next stage. It is important 'to plan ahead' and consider the tasks that potentially need to be completed next. Any early 'lessons learned' from the previous stage can be consolidated and incorporated into the next stage (Table 4.5).

4.4.2 Measuring the Innovation Phase (Gate 3 and 4)

New ideas need to be challenged and final tests need to be conducted in Gate 3 in accordance with our suggested Innovation Scorecard process model (Fig. 3.2, Sect. 3.3). Typically, tests need to focus on making sure that the chosen idea will work within the considered work area. For example, if the idea is to review and improve an existing work process, then it is imperative that the developed solution is tested as 'fit for intended purpose'. Testing, preferably in a 'live' environment, will provide the

Table 4.5 Gate 2 checklist

Stage 2 checklist

Category	Deliverable/activity	Owner	Tick if complete
Compulsory	Select final ideas	Initiative owner	
Compulsory	Produce 'proof of concept'	Initiative owner	
Essential	Obtain business sign off for each selected idea	Initiative owner	
Essential	Produce List of Deliverables and To Do list for team members	Initiative owner	
Essential	Initial testing	Initiative owner	
Essential	Prepare draft budget	Initiative owner	
Essential	Prepare risk assessment	Initiative owner	
Compulsory	Review and update the Project Definition Document (PDD)	Initiative owner	
Compulsory	Plan for the next stage	Initiative owner	

necessary evidence whether the idea can proceed to implementation or roll-out. Gate 3 assesses the idea's suitability and viability immediately prior to its implementation. The outcomes from Gate 1 and Gate 2 are considered and consolidated at Gate 3 to enable informed decision making before moving to Gate 4 (Fig. 3.2). Gate 4 takes a closer look at how well the chosen idea has performed during implementation. Actual performance is compared to forecasts. Assessed are also the strengths and weaknesses of the idea, in addition to 'end user satisfaction' and how well 'staff' accepted the idea into their existing working practices, for example.

Gate 3 Pre-implementation Planning

This section describes the steps associated with assessing new ideas' suitability, validity, and viability prior to launch. Its purpose is to:

- Conduct 'sanity' checks (Will the idea do what we think it will do?)
- Test that the idea works in a 'live' working environment
- Consolidate outcomes from Gate 1 and Gate 2
- Confirm that the idea can proceed to implementation
- Documentation and Plans
- Time Schedule
- Finalize Budget
- Key Stakeholder Support
- Produce metrics for use in Gate 4

- Update the Project Definition Document (PDD)
- Plan for the next stage

We suggest carrying out some 'sanity' checks before deciding whether to proceed with the implementation of a new idea or not. For example, if the idea is to improve an existing work process, it is possible to check the effectiveness of the process before and after the considered change. This is a kind of 'desk research' and is purely based on the idea's theoretical performance. Doing this in a 'non-live work environment' can provide valuable insights to help initiative owners decide whether the idea will meet expectations. In addition, the initiative owner needs to develop the test strategy from Gate 1 further and should consider the following:

- What are we going to test?
- Who is going to test?
- When/where are we going to test?
- What are we going to do with the test results?

The initiative owner needs to consider the need for any unit testing before integration or user acceptance testing is conducted. For example, before any testing such as a link or whole process is carried out, testing at the lowest level (unit) must be carried out successfully before moving on to the next level.

Any acquired knowledge and outcomes from previous Gates 1 and 2 can be considered and included in the review. This may include any concerns or negative feedback you may have had about the idea.

End user involvement and engagement is essential during this stage. Working closely with those who will ultimately apply and use the considered idea, is of paramount importance. It provides opportunities for early 'operational' feedback from the end user (s). This can then be incorporated into any potential solution redesign. The result will be a solution that works, is fit for its intended purpose and that has received 'buy-in' from end users.

It is essential to produce all relevant innovation initiative documentation and plans prior to implementation. We suggest producing a simple documentation register that shows all important issued documents including date, author, version, title, and a brief description of the content. Equally, producing a simple 'project plan' that contains all the details of the innovation initiative is highly desirable. In addition, producing a simple schedule of the work to be completed using a tool such as Microsoft Project should be considered. Both the documentation register and the schedule need to be reviewed at least monthly and kept up to date.

A final budget preparation needs to be conducted during Gate 3, updating the draft budget from Gate 2 appropriately. Efforts of work and any equipment or service costs should be reviewed and need to be updated to produce the final version of the budget for the planned innovation initiative.

We recommend that initiative owners should conduct a full stakeholder review and analysis at this stage to check if those who have a vested interest in the innovation initiative, are still committed to support the planned work. This can include financial support, providing the right resources at the right time and promoting their agreement to sponsor the innovation initiative across the business.

You need to develop and finalise appropriate metrics for your innovation initiative to measure how successful your change/innovation has been. Metrics measure 'set parameters' such as time, cost, and quality (Sect. 4.5). The setting of metrics is essential, for example, to any process of efficiency improvement. In selecting the metrics to gather, it is necessary to pass two simple tests:

- Is it measurable?
- Is it useful?

The descriptions in Sect. 4.5 will answer these questions and outline the relevance for statistical analysis.

Two more important steps need to be completed to finish this stage. The initiative owner should review and update the current version of the Project Definition Document (PDD) prior to launch. Agreed changes need to be included in the update in addition to any new requirements that have been added to scope. And finally, the initiative owner should take some time to think ahead and plan for the execution of the next gate (Table 4.6).

Table 4.6 Gate 3 checklist

Stage 3 checklist			
Category	Deliverable/activity	Owner	Tick if complete
Compulsory	Engage end users in the final idea design	Initiative owner	
Essential	Conduct a 'sanity' check-will the idea work?	Initiative owner	
Essential	Produce a draft list of metrics	Initiative owner	
Essential	Consolidate Gate 1 and Gate Outputs	Initiative owner	
Essential	Confirm that the idea is ready for implementation/roll out	Initiative owner	
Essential	Plans and Documentation	Initiative owner	
Essential	Finalise Budget	Initiative owner	
Essential	Key Stakeholder Support	Initiative owner	
Compulsory	Plan for the next stage	Initiative owner	
Compulsory	Review and update Project Definition Document (PDD)	Initiative owner	

Gate 4 Implementation and integration into Business as Usual (BAU)
This section describes the steps associated with the deployment of adopted ideas and their integration into daily business of the organisation (Business as Usual). Its purpose is to:

- Review and update the budget
- Focus on the completion of deliverables
- Manage team members
- Prepare for operational handover including all documentation
- Collect relevant data for use in the evaluation of applied metrics
- Review and update the Project Definition Document (PDD)
- Plan for the next stage

It is imperative to monitor all costs associated with the implementation of selected ideas. We suggest to regularly monitor the expenditure associated with any idea generation initiative. This frequency of the reviews depends on the complexity and size of your initiative. For some initiatives monthly appears to be sufficient, other initiatives may require weekly budget reviews. If the scope of work changes substantially, you may need to conduct 'budget reforecasts' to adjust financial requirements.

The list of deliverables produced in Gate 2 needs regular reviewing, too. Any list of deliverables is only as valid as the actions associated with it. In other words: it is what you do with the list that matters most, not so much that you simply have produced a list. Actions speak louder than words. This list needs to be reviewed at least monthly. It may be necessary to do this at more regular intervals such as weekly or fortnightly.

The initiative owner understands clearly what the innovation initiative is going to achieve. Taking time for the team to contribute to and understand the objectives which lead to greater commitment and better results. It is essential that the initiative owner fosters a good team spirit during the implementation stage to 'get the most out of people'. People who are committed, work better for the right reasons, and will continue to perform at the optimum for much longer.

When the initiative has been rolled out and implemented, the initiative owner needs to complete any issues and risks registers associated with the initiative. These need to be assessed following implementation and new owners need to be determined. This is usually done as part of the Post Implementation Review (Gate 5). The initiative owner must ensure that all relevant documentation suitably retained so it is available for future reference. We suggest the following options:

- Handover to operational units after the Post Implementation Review (Gate 5) has been completed
- Add to any organisations' Knowledge Management system
- Deposit in the organisation's archives

It is vital to collect regular performance data during this stage from those who are involved in the innovation initiative. This will help with checking, for example, the actual outcome versus the planned outcome and assist with gathering relevant data for any 'before' and 'after' statistical analysis. This data could be related to the measurement of (Sect. 4.5):

- Costs
- Variances on key plan parameters
- Earned Value
- Change Requests
- Staffing

As for Gate 3, two more important steps need to be completed to finish this stage. The initiative owner should review and update the current version of the Project Definition Document (PDD) prior to launch. Agreed changes need to be included in the update in addition to any new requirements that have been added to scope. And finally, the initiative owner should take some time to think ahead and plan for the execution of the next gate (Gate 5), including devising an initiative/project close-down/PIR plan.

The initiative owner/project manager needs to conduct a final budget review and update the budget before closing the initiative/project. The budget is now closed, and no further funding can be provided nor authorised (Table 4.7).

Table 4.7 Gate 4 checklist

Stage 4 checklist			
Category	Deliverable/activity	Owner	Tick if complete
Compulsory	Data Collection and Analysis	Initiative owner	
Essential	Completion of deliverables	Initiative owner	
Essential	Team Management	Initiative owner	
Essential	Prepare for Operational Handover	Initiative owner	
Essential	Update Project Definition Document (PDD)	Initiative owner	
Essential	Plan for next stage	Initiative owner	
Essential	Final Budget Update and Close Down	Initiative owner	

4.4.3   Closedown or Post Implementation Review (PIR) Phase (Gate 5)

This section describes the steps associated with the Closedown Stage, including mandatory activities and exit criteria. Its purpose is to:

- Implement the Closedown plan
- Hold PIR
- Capture the 'lessons learned' and what went well/what did not go well
- Write up and distribute the PIR review
- Develop 'benefits realisation summary'
- Remaining issues and risks assessed and closed down/handed over
- Gate 5 Approval
- Document 'retention requirements' set-up
- Close the initiative/project
- Celebrate success with the team

The purpose of the Closedown/PIR is to finish the initiative/project in a controlled manner (as specified in the approved closedown plan you produced towards the end of Gate 4). Activities include the release of staff, equipment de-commissioning, collection of statistics and storage for the retention of initiative/project documents.

An action plan for uncompleted deliverables is also required. The plan should also address on-going support required after the initiative/project has formally been closed.

The major activities for project completion are:

- Implementing the project closedown plan as approved at the PIR
- Managing documentation retention
- Review of initiative/project and implementation approach
- Development of the benefits realisation review plan
- Close initiative/project codes (where appropriate)

Projects that are wound up before completing the full Life Cycle must still go through Closedown, including the successful completion of Gate 5.

There are usually two Closedown criteria:

- Deployment complete
- The Gate Review of an earlier stage recommends Closedown.

Holding the Post Implementation Review
When all implantation/roll out activities are complete, or an initiative/project is wound up before completing its full Life Cycle, the initiative or project manager must hold a Post-Implementation Review (PIR). The purpose of the PIR is to:

- Compare the actual performance in terms of time, cost and quality with the Initiative or Project Definition Document (PDD, Sect. 4.2)
- Agree what worked well and what could have been improved
- Give those who are operating and maintaining the initiative/project deliverables—products, systems, or processes—valuable information about how they were designed and built
- review the remaining risks and issues and if necessary, hand these over to whoever is best placed to manage each one
- agree the project closedown plan

Writing the Post-implementation Report

A report should be written within 2 weeks of holding the PIR. The Post-Implementation Report documents the proceedings of the meeting as well as recording any recommendations made.

The Post-Implementation Report addresses all issues raised in the Project Definition Document. See Table 4.8 for the content of a Post-Implementation Report.

Copies of the Post-Implementation Report should be distributed to all those who have been involved with the project and would benefit from the information, whether internal or external. A copy of the PIR should be sent to relevant involved parties plus a copy should be deposited in your organisation's Knowledge Management system or 'shared drive' for use by the community of practice.

Table 4.8 Content of post-implementation report

Post-implementation report
Initiative/Project Background and Goal
Background
Goal
Objectives
Scope:
In Scope
Out of Scope
Work Breakdown Structure (WBS, Sect. 5.5)
Organisation
Milestones and Major Deliverables
Cost and Resource Requirements
Management System
Review Meetings
Reporting
Plans
Change Control
Issue Management
Risk Management
Assumptions, Constraints and Dependencies
User Perspectives and Comments

Developing the Benefits Realisation Summary

The initiative owner/project manager must produce a Benefits Realisation Summary. The purpose of the summary is to establish the mechanisms by which the success of the initiative/project deliverables can be assessed. For a product development or improvement initiative/project, for example, the mechanisms may include the collection of subscriber connections, usage, and churn (turn over) statistics over a 12-month period. This data can then be compared with the forecasts made in the PDD (Sect. 4.2).

Assessment and Hand over of Remaining Issues and Risks

The initiative/project owner ensures that the Issues and Risks registers are updated following the PIR, where they are assessed. Appropriate 'owners' for any outstanding issues and risks are determined. Any issue management documentation and risks mitigation plans should be provided to these new 'owners'.

Gate 5 Approval

To progress through Gate 5 and formally closedown the initiative/project, the initiative/project owner must complete a Gate 5 Paper (Appendix H). Where there is a project manager (rather than an initiative owner), the completed form must be submitted to any Project Review Board/PMO that may, overall, oversee all internal projects. Otherwise, the initiative owner should send the completed Gate 5 Paper to the initiative sponsor.

Setting-up the Document Retention Requirements

The initiative owner/project manager must ensure that all relevant documentation is suitably retained so it is available for future reference. It is recommended that the company's archives be used for this purpose. The initiative owner/project manager must provide details of where the documents are stored, for example, to any Knowledge Management co-ordinator so that the information can be accessed and moved to any Knowledge Management System.

Project Closure

When the Gate 5 Plan has been successfully completed the project is closed.

Post Implementation Celebration

At the end of a successful initiative/project, the initiative owner/project manager should arrange for a celebration with the team (Table 4.9).

4.5   Innovation Metrics

As briefly described in Gate 3, the term 'metric', in this context, means measurable initiative/project parameters. These range from costs to how many staff walked out during the initiative/project. The primary reason for gathering metrics is that they be subjected to statistical analysis. We consider that the gathering of metrics is essential

Table 4.9 Gate 5 checklist

Stage 5 checklist

Category	Deliverable/activity	Owner	Tick if complete
Compulsory	Implement Closedown Plan	Initiative owner	
Compulsory	Hold PIR	Initiative owner	
Compulsory	Write and Distribute PIR Report to appropriate Audience	Initiative owner	
Essential	Issues and Risks Handed over	Initiative owner	
Essential	Benefits Realisation Plan Produced and Distributed	Initiative owner	
Essential	Gate 5 Closedown Approval	Initiative owner	
Essential	Document Retention Set up	Initiative owner	
Nice to have	Post Implementation Celebration with Team	Initiative owner	

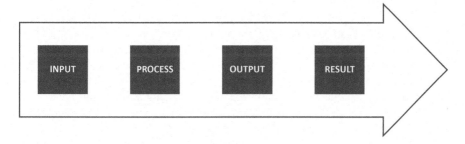

Fig. 4.2 The input–process–output–result model (ISO, 2021)

to any process of work efficiency improvement. Perfect for measuring, for example, how successful something has been.

Our adopted metric approach is based on the current ISO 9001: 2015 Standard (reviewed in 2021). To capture the causal relationships behind an innovation and how to measure 'how successful the innovation has been', our Innovation Scorecard builds on the ISO 9001: 2015 Standard 'input–process–output–result' model (Fig. 4.2). Working to the ISO 9001: 2015 Standard enabled us to achieve good guidance on how to monitor and manage trends through the application of key performance metrics to enhance performance through innovation. The ISO 9001: 2015 Standard offers another benefit. It provides appropriate advice how to improve business performance constructively.

Inputs are the resources devoted to the 'innovation effort'. This means using the quantity and quality of the inputs dedicated to the operation as a proxy of its performance. Possible inputs include tangible elements such as people, money, equipment, office space, and time, but also intangibles such as motivation and company culture. Inputs are leading measures of success.

Processes combine the inputs and transform them. Typical processes are idea generation, new product development, project selection, and technology acquisition, whereas characteristic indicators are the average product life cycle length, the average time of redesign, and the percentage of initiatives/projects that do not meet established schedules, target costs or standard of professionalism, in relation to, for example, the capability to create professional documentations and establish successful cooperation with partners. They are real-time measures (meaning that they measure current activities) and track the progress toward creating outputs. Process measures are critical during execution because they can signal the need to change course or alter the execution.

Outputs are the results of innovation efforts. Output measures describe what the innovation efforts have delivered. These measures are 'lagging' measures. Efforts need to be completed first before they can be measured 'how successful they have been'. Output measures describe key characteristics such as whether the company has superior innovation performance, more effective customer acquisition, or better customer loyalty.

Results describe value creation and **Outputs** describe quality, quantity, and timeliness. Results provide evidence of how the innovation effort translated the outputs into value for the company and the net amount of the value contribution. If the output of a particular innovation initiative/project is successful and profitable for the company, the result will yield positive outcomes. However, a similar initiative/project could produce the same quality and quantity of innovation outputs, but not lead to value creation. It may have missed the market window of opportunity, or the innovation characteristics delivered may not have been as powerful in attracting consumers as had been anticipated. In this case, the result would be negative, at least in the sense of commercial viability. Valuable learning outcomes from the initiative/project still may have made it worthwhile, despite the cost. Examples are average cost reductions, percentage of sales from new products, or degree of product improvements.

A typical list of metrics for each gate can then look as follows (see four samples below for ideas for potential metrics and associated performance measurements in Appendices D–G) (Table 4.10):

Table 4.10 An Innovation Scorecard matrix

	Metric	Unit	Target	Actual	Variance	Owner
Inputs	Metric 1	...	...	...	...	...
Process	Metric 2	...	...	...	...	...
	Metric 3	...	...	...	...	...
Outputs	Metric 4	...	...	...	...	...
Results	Metric 5	...	...	...	...	...

The following process descriptions will answer the two previously mentioned questions and outline the relevance for statistical analysis. This is not a finite list of sample metrics but rather a starting point to get you on the right track to design and develop metrics together with business unit managers that will be fit for your intended purpose.

Costs
The measurement of costs can be broken down into three areas:

- Internal Costs and variance to schedule
- Equipment Costs and variance to schedule
- Supplier Costs and variance to schedule

The need to acquire these numbers should be self-evident. However, they are also pre-requisites for some of the metrics that follow (see Appendices I and J).

Variances on key plan parameters
Four metrics are of interest here:

- Variance on schedule (go live target date)
- Variance on schedule and cost to go live
- Plan is original target. Cost variance compared to Gate 3
- Plan to original target, go live variance compared to Gate 3

All expressed in % terms. Gathering these metrics over a statistically significant sample of projects will enable a judgment to be made about:

- The basis on which initiatives/projects are initiated
- The reliability of the estimating process

Earned Value
Earned value is a technique that applies at intermediate initiative/project stages, milestones, or gates. The objective is to judge how far along the road the initiative/project is and at what cost. This is then compared with expected. The available data directs that this is a 'date variance' driven metric.

Ultimately it may be possible to investigate effort/spend profiles in this way. At this stage it is proposed merely to gather the variance on planned dates at milestones and gates. Initiatives/projects involving suppliers, particularly fixed price contracts, are very likely to incorporate key milestones in the planning process. All Innovation Scorecard initiatives/projects have gates. The statistical significance of this is that it can be used to determine the weighting between the project phases and identify those areas where estimate unreliability exists, leading to targeted improvements.

Change Requests

Change requests are very interesting in terms of establishing why initiatives/projects deliver, or not. Any extended statistical analysis will be interested in a measure of requirement stability and the quality of the initial assumptions (Appendix K). All change requests should have a tabulated entry that indicates the following:

Impact:

- Major
- Minor
- Trivial

Two entries: cost and time 'to go live'. Absolutes, not %.
Requirements:

- Did it result from a change in requirement? Y/N

Technology Issue:

- Is it to take advantage of improved technology? Y/N
- Is it a result of proposed technology either failing, or not being understood? Y/N

Forced:

- Was it taken under control as desirable, or was it forced? Y/N

Scope:

- Did it entail a variance in scope? Yes/No

Staffing

People delivering an initiative/project are an essential factor in general management. Team stability is associated with initiative/project success. Staff changes are a desirable metric to be gathered for comparison against successful initiatives/projects (Appendix L). Three metrics should be considered:

- Planned Staff Changes. Key-Y/N, Total. Dates (to identify clusters around key events)
- Unplanned Staff Changes. Key-Y/N Total. Dates (to identify clusters around key events)
- No Shows. Positions that were never filled. Key-Y/N Total.

Return on Investment

Put simply, the so-called Return on Investment (ROI) is a ratio between net income and investment. A high ROI means that the investment has a good return compared

Table 4.11 Gate 5 checklist

Stage 5 checklist

Category	Deliverable/activity	Owner	Tick if complete
Compulsory	Metric Form/List	Initiative owner	
Essential	Conduct suitability Tests	Initiative owner	
Essential	Prepare Input, Output, Process and Result details for each metric	Initiative owner	
Essential	Develop and agree metrics with business unit manager(s)	Initiative owner	

to the associated costs. The efficiency of, for example, an innovation can be measured to prove whether the innovation has been successful or not.

The principle is that any ROI should be compared with any ROI that was set as a performance metric, predicted at the outset of the initiative/project. The desirability of this is self-evident. To achieve this, it is essential that a metricated business case exists for future comparison (including any business case).

Initiative owners/project managers should, with the help of a financial specialist (usually finance manager), check the actual outcome against the planned outcome. If your business delivers programmes, then 'programme managers' can evaluate this information with initiative owners/project managers so that the accuracy of business plans/cases can be improved (Table 4.11).

4.6   Innovation Scorecard Data Sheet

Once the initiative owner/project manager has agreed a set of performance metrics for each of the gates, it is necessary to design and develop the selected characteristics for each metric. Figure 4.3 presents a suggested example of an 'Innovation Scorecard Data Sheet' template. Its aim is to demonstrate what a good and solid performance metric needs to contain. (Niven, 2014). We recommend producing this sheet for any considered innovation project/initiative. It is a useful tool that helps 'the owner' to clearly define and develop appropriate 'metrics' that are 'fit for their intended purpose'. Inputs should be based on defined formulas and data sources that are appropriate for what you need to have in place. A little bit of 'tweaking' here and there will be necessary depending on requirements. The following details should be included (detailed descriptions for the various headings are provided in the short sections that follow Fig. 4.3 below):

- Background details for each metric
- Specific metric characteristics and measurements
- Calculations and data specifications

Gate: .... Phase:	Measure number/name: .... Owner: ....
Strategy:	Goal: ....
Definition:	

Lag/Lead: .... Frequency:	Unit Type: .... Polarity: ....

Formula:	
Data source:	
Data quality:	Data collector: ....

Baseline:	Target: ....
Target rationale:	Initiatives: ....

Fig. 4.3 Innovation Scorecard data sheet template

Measurement Background

Perspective-what perspective drives the metric (financial/customer/internal process/innovation/business growth).

Gate-shows the initiative's/project's current gate for which the metric will be applied.

Phase-shows the metric's phase (input/process/output/result)

Measure Number/Name-all performance measures should be numbered and uniquely named, using a meaningful title. A good name is one that explains what the measure is and why it is important. It should be self-explanatory and not include any jargon.

Strategy-shows a clear link between strategy and metric.

Goal-explain how the metric will contribute towards achieving any set goal (s) and why it was chosen.

Owner-identify the person who will be responsible and accountable for the results.

Description-provide a brief, clear and unambiguous description of the metric.

Measure Characteristics

Lag/Lead-assess and state whether the initiative/project metric is an outcome indicator (change) or a performance driver (benchmark or competitive pressure)

Frequency-decide how frequently you will record, and report progress made (daily, fortnightly, or monthly.

Unit Type-decide how you will present the metric as 'measurement units' such as numbers, percentages, or monetary (€, $, £).

Polarity-conduct a viability assessment: for example, do high performance values indicate good outcomes? Do low performance values indicate bad outcomes?

Calculation and Data Specifications

Formula-present any chosen 'equation' that performs a calculation here, such as $(B-A)/A*100$ (A = planned cost; B = actual cost), to calculate the percentage variance to a baseline schedule.

Data Source-state the source of all applied data to aid 'performance comparison over time'.

Data Quality-comment on the quality of the applied data (is it generated automatically or verbally?)

Data Collector-state who is responsible for the collection of all metric data.

Performance Information

Baseline-baseline metrics once the performance measures have been agreed with business unit owners.

Target-establish metric target values during Gate 2 and track progress regularly such as weekly, fortnightly, or monthly.

Target Rationale-state your rational thinking behind the chosen metric targets.

Initiatives-map any current or specific initiatives/projects to specific metrics.

References

Association for Project Management. (2019). *Body of knowledge* (7th ed.). Association for Project Management (APM).

Bessant, J., & Tidd, J. (2011). *Innovation and entrepreneurship*. Wiley.

Cooper, R. G. (2008). Perspective: The Stage-Gate idea-to-launch process – update, What's new and NextGenSystems. *Journal of Product Innovation Management, 25*, 213–232.

Davila, T., Epstein, M. J., & Shelton, R. D. (2013). *Making innovation work: How to manage it, measure it, and profit from it*. FT Press.

Doerr, J. (2018). *Measure what matters: How Google, Bono, and the Gates Foundation rock the world with OKRs*. Pengiun.

International Standards Organisation (ISO). (2021). [on-line]. Accessed June 10, 2021, from https://www.iso.org

Niven, P. R. (2014). *Balanced Scorecard evolution: A dynamic approach to strategy execution*. Wiley.

Skarzynski, P., & Gibson, R. (2008). *Innovation to the core: A blueprint for transforming the way your company innovates*. Harvard Business Press.

Thomaschewski, D., & Tarlatt, A. (2010). Determinants for failure and success in innovation management. In *Innovation and international corporate growth*. Springer.

Tidd, J., Bessant, J. R., & Pavitt, K. (2005). *Managing innovation: Integrating technological, market and organizational change*. Wiley.

Tools and Techniques

5

Our suggested Tools and Techniques are based on current industry 'best practice' and the Association for Project Management's (APM) Body of Knowledge (BoK), 7th edition, published in 2019. The APMBoK provides an authoritative statement on project management and the foundations on which the profession is built. It should be considered as a starting point providing knowledge and understanding of key concepts in project management. It serves as a reference and method for more experienced professionals, too. The presented tools and techniques have been modified to suit both 'initiatives and projects' associated with measuring how successful innovations or changes have been. They act as guidelines and not finite solutions and should be modified to suit individual needs.

5.1 Kick-Off Meeting

A Kick-off Meeting or Initiative/Project Definition Workshop (PDW) should be held for every project at the end of Gate 2 or at the beginning of Gate 3. The Initiative Owner/Project Manager is responsible for organising the workshop. Representatives from the initiative/project, including the Initiative Sponsor/Project Owner, as well as key team members, should attend the meeting. Normally, the Initiative Owner/ Project Manager runs the PDW, but might prefer to use an independent facilitator.

The PDW is essentially a structured discussion to achieve the following:

- To confirm the objectives and deliverables of the Initiative/Project
- To confirm the commitment of the Initiative or Project Sponsor, and other key stakeholders and team members
- To achieve a common understanding of the purpose and approach for the initiative/project
- To agree how the initiative/project is to be managed
- To provide a firm agreed base for planning
- To provide initial cost and resource estimates

© The Author(s), under exclusive license to Springer Nature Switzerland AG 2021
O. Zizlavsky, E. Fisher, *Innovation Scorecard*, Management for Professionals,
https://doi.org/10.1007/978-3-030-82688-8_5

- To provide an assessment of risks, issues, and dependencies
- To decide how to measure progress and what to do with the information obtained

Initiative/Project Definition Workshop Guidelines
Preparation: Use the preparation for the PDW as an opportunity to get your thoughts clear and to save time at the meeting. Discuss workshop topics in advance and construct a framework for the meeting. This provides a starting point for discussion during the workshop.

Agenda: A standard agenda for the PDW is:

- Initiative/Project Goals—define and confirm the goals
- Objectives—clear statements of the aims of the initiative/project, enabling the following questions to be answered:
  - Is this in line with business objectives? What have we got to achieve?
  - How will we know when we have finished?
  - How will we know that we have done well?
  - When has the initiative/project got to complete the tasks?
  - How much will the initiative/project cost?

Scope: The scope defines or clarifies the boundaries within which the objectives of the initiative/project will be met, to ensure it is working to achievable limits. It may be helpful also to identify things that are out of scope.

Work Breakdown Structure (WBS): The basis for the schedule and indicates what needs to be done (see Sect. 5.5).

Organisation and Resource Requirements (including initial cost estimates): The management structure and organisation of the initiative/project must be clearly defined. Resources required to run the initiative/project must also be identified (by name if possible) and a commitment obtained to provide these resources (either directly or raised as an issue with an action to resolve within a short time). The roles, responsibilities, and scope of involvement for everyone on an initiative/project team. Initial cost estimates should be available before the PDW so they can be collated and discussed at the meeting. If the cost estimates are not available before the PDW, they should be derived as far as possible during the workshop and the actions assigned so that full cost estimates can be included in the PDD. The level of confidence in all estimates should be stated.

Milestones and major Deliverables: A list of the major initiative/project deliverables and target milestone dates should be produced.

Manage the Initiative/Project Plan: The management system helps to ensure things go to plan, stating how the initiative/project will be reviewed, how risks, issues and problems will be managed, and how changes will be controlled.

Assumptions, constraints, and dependencies: Any assumptions and constraints should be identified, and their impact understood. Where appropriate, external dependencies should be identified, and actions put in place to agree these with the owning functions.

Risks: A list of risks to the success of the initiative/project should be drawn up along with a plan to mitigate the effect of these risks. Generally, each risk will be assigned an Owner who must assess it and develop mitigation plans. This forms the basis of the Initiative/Project Risk Register (Sect. 5.4).

Immediate Issues and Actions: A list of immediate issues will have emerged during the workshop. What should be done to resolve them (and by whom), and any other actions, should be agreed at the end of the PDW. This forms the basis of the Initiative/Project Issues Register (adapt the Initiative/Project Risk Register template from Sect. 5.4 (Appendix O) and convert it into an Issues Register). These actions should be followed up by the Initiative/Project Manager after the PDW.

Initiative/Project Definition Document (PDD, Sect. 4.4.1)
The outcome from the PDW is agreement on the way forward. This is documented in the Project Definition Document (PDD, Appendix B). It is written by the initiative/project manager. The document's content and structure maps directly to the topics covered in the PDW. This Document must be circulated after the workshop to all participants. The Initiative Owner/Sponsor must approve the PDD, and preferably it should be signed off by all divisions or departments involved.

It may be helpful to prepare a draft of the PDD in advance of the PDW as a working document for the participants, provided this is positioned as a proposal for the Workshop, rather than a rubber-stamping exercise.

The PDD is the central document relating to the definition and management of the initiative/project. Its objectives are:

- To provide a written record of the PDW agreement
- To confirm the deliverables of the initiative/project
- To confirm the commitment of the Initiative Owner or Sponsor
- To provide a firm agreed base for planning
- To provide an initial estimate of cost and resources required

The PDD describes what is to be done and when, how and by whom it will be done. Some of the sections may simply be references to the location of more detailed information on this subject. This is particularly relevant for items, which will change regularly, such as Risks and Issues. It means the PDD does not need re-issue each time they change.

The PDD includes sections defining the principal initiative/project deliverables. For each deliverable this should state acceptance criteria (proof of concept) and sign-off procedures. It may not be possible to finalise these during Gate 2 but the earlier they are agreed, the lower the risk of them being not met or compromised.

Although the PDD is initially produced following the PDW, the Initiative/Project Manager should update and reissue the PDD at the start of each subsequent stage, and if appropriate from time to time in between (for example when significant changes are agreed).

5.2   Stage Review

The authors suggest that this Stage Review Procedure must be followed at the end of every stage during the Life Cycle of your innovation initiative.

Objectives
The main objectives of a Stage Review are:

- To determine whether all exit criteria defined in the Project Definition Document (PDD) have been achieved for the given stage, and that deliverables are traceable and support the original requirements.
- To authorise subsequent stages to start (or to continue if the stages overlap).
- To initiate corrective action where exit criteria have not been met.

Stage reviews also provide a formal mechanism for reviewing the initiative/project against current business objectives. While a given stage may have been completed in line with time, cost and quality objectives, the business environment may have changed. Stage reviews therefore provide an opportunity to evaluate the following:

- Are the original initiative/project assumptions still correct?
- Is the budget still valid?
- Is the business priority still appropriate?

Scope
All registered initiatives/projects are subject to Stage Reviews.

Procedure
Stage Review Team
  The stage review team comprises:

- Reviewed—Initiative owner/project manager (with support from initiative/project team if appropriate)
- Reviewer(s)—Reviewing body—typically the Owner and Steering Group (where one has been established, depending on the size and complexity of the initiative/project)
- Approver(s)—Approval body—typically Senior Management/Director/CEO

Stage Review Inputs and Outputs
  Mandatory inputs and outputs for all stage reviews are defined below. There may be specific additional items defined in the Project Definition Document (PDD).
  Inputs:

- Completed stage review procedure
- Evidence to demonstrate that each of the exit criteria has been met.

Outputs:

- Completion of Stage Review Form
- Action plan

Process:

- During initiative/project definition, the initiative/project life cycle and the review body for each stage are identified.

At the beginning of each stage, the initiative owner/project manager must confirm and document the exit criteria for the stage. This will normally be done when a new stage is launched. We suggest that the owner should hold a 'stage launch meeting' with relevant parties to discuss and agree what will be done during the next stage.

The Stage Review date must be included as a milestone in the signed off plan. The agenda for the review should be agreed with the appropriate parties.

The initiative owner/project manager is responsible for the production, quality assurance, review and approval off all deliverables and stage exit criteria for each life cycle stage.

Towards the end of the stage the initiative owner/project manager must prepare for the review and collate all required documentation and other evidence to demonstrate that the exit criteria have been met. Outputs can be used for presentation to any existing review board as required.

Stage Reviews follow a standard agenda (Presentation and review of stage exit criteria and supporting evidence):

- Project Status (planned vs actual at this checkpoint)
- Timescales
- Costs
- Deliverables
- Major Risks and Issues
- Plans for next stage/rest of initiative/project
- Review and confirmation of continued initiative/project justification.

The decision of the Reviewer leads to one of four outcomes:

- Proceed: All exit criteria met—proceed to next stage.
- Proceed but . . .: Some further work required, but initiative/project can proceed subject to agreement of corrective actions. A re-review may be required in this case.
- Hold: Serious problems with initiative/project and/or exit criteria. Initiative/project cannot proceed until problems resolved. A Re-review is mandatory in this case.
- Close: The initiative/project is no longer achievable and/or justifiable—initiative/project closed.

The decision is confirmed on a Stage Review Form (Appendix M). The form is prepared by the initiative owner/project manager and signed off by the reviewer. It should be retained in the initiative/project file.

Where further detail is required, minutes of the review may also be produced summarising the basis of the decisions taken and listing any required actions.

5.3   Monitoring and Control: Reporting and Reviewing

To achieve the principal objective of completing the initiative/project on Time, to Cost and with the required Quality, the initiative owner/project manager must monitor progress and control resources. Therefore, reporting and reviewing progress are crucial parts of the initiative's/project manager's job, to ensure that tasks are proceeding according to the schedule. Any deviations from planned progress should be investigated and explained.

Initiative/project control involves:

• Measuring progress against the plan, budget, and specification
• Evaluating the impact of any variances
• Determining an appropriate course of corrective action (Table 5.1).

Reporting Progress
One of the aims of initiative/project management is to highlight problems and issues early in the process and take appropriate action to lessen their impact. The earlier the action, the less likely the initiative/project is to be adversely affected.

When the initiative/project is initiated, the initiative owner/project manager, with guidance from any steering group, should decide how to measure progress and what to do with the information obtained. This should be documented with a schedule of progress reviews, stating exactly who is involved in each, in the Project Definition Document (PDD).

Table 5.1 Monitoring and control checklist

Monitoring and control checklist			
Meetings	Owner	Frequency	Tick if complete
Management Board (where applicable)	Initiative Owner/Project Manager	Quarterly	
Review Board for Gate Approvals	Project Review Board Chairman	Regularly, when required	
Initiative/Project Review	Initiative Owner/Project Manager	Monthly	
Functional Reviews	Work Stream Leader/Sprint Teams (SCRUM)	Regularly/weekly as required	
And others to meet your individual needs...			

It is important to remember the inter-relationship of Time, Cost and Quality, and to aim to measure tangible achievement: 'What has been delivered?' means more than 'How much money has been spent'. Concepts such as earned value give a more objective view of progress.

Prior to the progress review, a report may be prepared and circulated to those attending. It should be of a standard format and cover, at a minimum:

- Status (written summary)
- Progress against milestones
- Issues, risks, changes, and dependencies.

In addition, reports such as 'Schedules of Work' produced directly from planning tools may be prepared.

Reviewing Progress

Progress reviews are an essential part of the initiative/project management process. They are structured and formal reviews, which are scheduled to take place at regular intervals throughout the initiative/project.

Progress reviews take place at different levels within the initiative/project structure and are designed to ensure progress is monitored against plans at all levels and that any issues/risks arising are addressed and resolved, or escalated, in good time. In particular, the review should aim to root out problems and highlight danger areas. **The initiative owner/project manager must never be in the position of only finding out a target has been missed after reaching the relevant milestone in the schedule.**

When considering completed tasks, the review should seek tangible evidence that deliverables have been handed over and acceptance criteria met.

No individual should need to have the same work reviewed more than once, so every initiative/project needs to establish a review schedule compatible with its structure.

Runaway Initiatives/Projects

Sometimes, despite following our suggested methodology, initiative owners/project managers may lose control of the initiative/project and must seek a course of action to try and rescue it.

Very importantly, the initiative owner/project manager must not hide failures to make things look better than they are. The smaller the variance from the plan, the less costly will be the corrective action; the cost of collecting something that has gone wrong rises sharply if it is left unresolved.

In such cases, it is sensible for initiative owners/project managers to discuss problems with their sponsor, or to seek advice and assistance from other experienced colleagues.

Changing a Schedule

As the initiative/project proceeds, the schedule will probably need to be amended following changes in requirements, deliverables, and so on, or to recover lost ground. Changes to plans may arise:

- Following approval of a formal Change Request (Sect. 5.6)
- After authorisation by a progress review meeting/stage review (Sect. 5.2)
- By agreement with the initiative/project sponsor

Such changes will require action and impact analysis in all affected areas, and these must be specified in a formal memo or minutes. The revised schedule will serve as a communication aid to inform task owners of changes to start/finish dates or task content.

There will also be times when the initiative owner/project manager will wish to make minor changes to the schedule (for example, those which do not affect deliverables or milestones). Before making any changes the initiative owner/project manager must be satisfied that there are/will be no impact on other initiatives/ projects, or resource issues relating to those changes.

5.4   Risk Management

Introduction

The last few sections have described methods, tools, and techniques for managing initiatives/projects to performance parameters such as time, cost, and quality. We shall now consider the management of risks inherent in these.

Initiatives/projects are by nature uncertain. The uncertainty is normally identified in terms of risks, or threats, to the success of the initiative/project; it is not possible even with the most accurate estimates and detailed plans to eliminate risk from an initiative owner's/project manager's agenda. Therefore, the initiative owner/project manager needs to manage the risks associated with their work. They need to make assumptions about future performance. This introduces an element of uncertainty.

A risk is a potential event or set of circumstances which has both uncertainty and loss associated with it. In an initiative/project context it is something that might happen and, if it does, will adversely affect the outcome of the planned work: it might be late, the budget might be over-spent, the deliverables might not meet the specification, or the initiative/project might fail completely.

This Section explains our recommended risk management approach that you can apply in your initiative/project. For smaller projects, this approach can be modified to suit your individual needs and to align it to the complexity of your initiative/ project. In either case, the initiative owner/project manager must set up a risk register to capture all considered associated and identified risks relating to the planned work.

Taking active steps to reduce the possible effects of risks is not indicative of pessimism but is a positive indication of good, effective management.

Risk management starts when the initiative/project starts. It reduces the likelihood of threats materializing but the initiative owner/project manager should plan for contingencies if threats do materialise. Focus on the 'big ones' but do not lose sight of the others.

An initiative/project should not usually contain any high risks when first planned. If it does the initiative/project plan/schedule should be reconsidered to lower the overall risk by using an alternative approach or by introducing ways of reducing the likely impact.

Risk Management Overview

Risk management provides a systematic approach to identifying, assessing, and managing risks so that initiative owners/project managers can limit the impact of occurrences which can throw an initiative/project off track. Risk management has four main elements.

- Identifying risks and the options for minimising their impact
- Analysing each risk by estimating the probability of it occurring and the impact (in terms of Time, Cost and Quality) on the planned work if it does occur, hence deciding which risks are significant
- Producing a plan for mitigating significant risks
- Monitoring the risks throughout the planned work, including identification and management of new risks (Table 5.2)

The Benefits of Risk Management

Taking active steps to reduce the possible effects of risks is not indicative of pessimism but is a positive indication of good, effective management.

Risk management offers:

Increased probability of success through facing up to realities and focusing on key threats

More objective investment decisions by providing better assessments of intangible initiative/project benefits:

- Avoidance of 'no-win' initiatives/projects by identifying cases where risks outweigh benefits
- Increased team motivation through realistic (achievable) targets, more planned and less reactive working, and shared problem-solving amongst all team members
- Improved customer satisfaction and confidence by making initiative/project deliverables more predictable
- Improvement in the management of future initiatives/projects through the availability of historic data and documentation.

Risk management can also provide opportunities for additional business benefits by giving the Project Manager a framework within which to take deliberate risks.

However, initiative/project managers should concentrate primarily on developing techniques for mitigating or removing adverse risks.

Table 5.2 Risk management checklist

Risk management checklist

Category	Deliverable/activities	Owner	Tick if complete
Compulsory	Identify Risks at PDW	Initiative Owner/Project Manager	
Essential	Issue invitations to representatives from involved parties to Risk Assessment Workshop or, as a minimum, engage in the risk assessment process	Initiative Owner/Project Manager	
Essential	Arrange for a facilitator (if applicable)	Initiative Owner/Project Manager	
Essential	Define scope and objectives of workshop.	Initiative Owner/Project Manager	
Essential	Issue PDD to workshop participants for background.	Initiative Owner/Project Manager	
Compulsory	Issue risk identification starter list (see Appendix N) to participants.	Initiative Owner/Project Manager	
Essential	Run workshop.	Initiative Owner/Project Manager	
Essential	List risks.	Initiative Owner/Project Manager	
Essential	Identify area of impact.	All workshop participants	
Essential	Assess probability and impact.	All workshop participants	
Essential	Summarise in risk exposure matrix.	Initiative Owner/Project Manager	
Compulsory	Prioritise significant risks.	Initiative Owner/Project Manager	
Essential	Assign Owners.	Initiative Owner/Project Manager	
Essential	Set up risk register.	Initiative Owner/Project Manager	
Essential	Produce risk mitigation plan.	Initiative Owner/Project Manager	

(continued)

Table 5.2 (continued)

Risk management checklist

Category	Deliverable/activities	Owner	Tick if complete
Essential	Add risk-related activities to initiative/ project plan.	Initiative Owner/Project Manager	
Compulsory	Monitor high priority risks monthly.	Initiative Owner/Project Manager	
Essential	Monitor lower priority risks regularly.	Initiative Owner/Project Manager	

Type of Risk

Most risks fall into one of the following categories:

- Technical
- Financial
- Commercial
- Regulatory or political
- Operational/Maintenance
- Environmental

The following are examples of areas of risk:

- Newly developed equipment, software, or work processes
- New supplier (s)
- Requirements more exacting than before
- Activities requiring new or scarce skills: training will need to be provided
- Dependencies on other initiatives/projects
- Availability of appropriate test environment (s)
- Procurement and Supply Chain Management (for example, single sourcing)

Principles of Risk Analysis

The initiative owner/project manager should balance the effort expended in properly mitigating identified risks against the value of avoiding the impact of the risk. This requires two factors to be assessed quantitively:

- The probability of the risk materialising (measured as a percentage)
- The impact in terms of Time, Cost and Quality if it does materialise, (measured as a variance from the target).

Table 5.3 Risk
categorisation matrix

Probability		Impact	
High	>70%	High	>15%
Medium	30–70%	Medium	5–15%
Low	<30%	Low	<5%

Table 5.4 Risk matrix—
example

Identified risk	P	S	D	RPN
1) Bad Weather	3	2	4	24
2) Loss of Key Team Member	2	8	8	128
3) Technology will not work	6	10	8	480

For most initiatives/projects it is sufficient to adopt a High-Medium-Low categorisation, as shown below (Table 5.3). The figures here are for illustration purposes.

The initiative owner/project manager then decides which risks are significant and so need a formal mitigation plan. The criteria for determining significance will vary but, as a guide, any risk which scores 'HIGH' on either probability or impact (or both) or one that scores 'MEDIUM' on both, should be regarded as significant.

Initiative owners/project managers must prioritise risks so that the most important ones are worked on rather than waste time on less significant risks.

An alternative method is to assess the probability of a risk only by using a method known as that Risk Probability Number (RPN).

The severity of the effect is assessed on a scale from hazardous; project severely impacted; possible cancellation; ranked at 10, to no severity; no effect, ranked 1.

The detection capability is assessed on a scale from absolute uncertainty, ranked at 10, to almost certain, ranked 1.

For each risk the initiative owner/project manager has identified three measures: a probability level, a severity measure, and a detection capability. These three numbers are multiplied to obtain a risk probability number (RPN). To show how this works, consider the three risks shown below (Table 5.4).

In this example, severity for bad weather is so small it can be ignored. However, the other two RPNs are significantly high. Example 2 has a low probability (2) but a high severity and high detection. **A suggested general rule: wherever severity is high,** *regardless of the RPN,* **special attention should be given to this task**.

Risk Mitigation
The initiative owner/project manager should produce a mitigation plan for all the significant risks for approval by the initiative/project sponsor. Possible mitigation approaches include:

• Avoidance: remove the risk entirely by changing the initiative/project, for example, by using a different platform or replanning over a different time frame; this is usually only a viable option in the early stages of an initiative/project.

- Probability reduction: reduce the likelihood of the risk occurring, for example, by not scheduling testing at a time when the business is already going live with many new products and test resources will be 'stretched'.
- Impact reduction: reduce the impact if the risk does happen, for example. by building redundancy into a 'test network'.
- Contingency: update the planning estimates to include extra money and/or time in plans and budgets as a provision against the consequences of the risk if it occurs (for example, to employ extra staff or to buy more equipment).

Risk Assessment Workshop

An effective way of developing risk mitigation plans is to hold a risk assessment workshop.

For smaller initiatives/projects, risks can be assessed during the Project Definition Workshop (PDW).

The workshop should be attended by the initiative owner/project manager, the sponsor, team member(s) with relevant expertise, other technical experts and representatives from each function contributing to the initiative/project. A trained facilitator may be used.

The scope and the objectives for the workshop need to be set in advance and all participants should understand the initiative's/project's goals, objectives, constraints and assumptions (defined after the PDW in the Project Definition Document–Sect. 4. 4.1, Appendix B).

Risk Identification starter list

Appendix N presents some 'risk identification starter' lists. This covers various risk types. These are examples only and each initiative owner/project manager should prepare a list appropriate to a given initiative/project.

Risk Register

Our suggested risk registration form can be found in Appendix O. If an initiative owner/project manager wishes to adopt a different method of risk registration (for example a spreadsheet) this must include at least the information on the recommended form. Where an alternative method is used this must be documented in the initiative/project file.

Risk Mitigation Plan

We recommend that you should set up, for each significant risk, an individual risk mitigation plan. A form for recording this plan can be found in Appendix P. If an initiative owner/project manager wishes to adopt a different method of mitigating planning (for example a spreadsheet), then this must include at least the information on the recommended form. Where an alternative method is used this must be documented in the initiative/project file.

Monitoring Risks

Risk monitoring involves identifying any changes in risk status and revising the plan if necessary, ensuring changes are carried through into other plans and documents.

As the severity of a risk changes over time, high priority risks should be monitored at weekly progress reviews. Lower priority risks should be monitored by their owner and reviewed at least monthly at a progress review.

Monitoring should be done on a regular basis, but special reviews may be required if certain trigger conditions arise. Risk review should be a standard initiative/project management activity and on the agenda for every progress review meeting.

New risks should be identified as they arise, analysed and added to the plan.

Dealing with Risks That Materialise

Risks are 'uncertainties' by definition. They rarely materialise suddenly. In practice, catastrophic events will not have been identified as significant risks and so will not be covered in the mitigation plans. Therefore, the initiative owner/project manager will normally have a clear response—normally some specific, planned actions—for dealing with the event when it happens.

The mitigation plan activities are incorporated into the main initiative/project plan.

It may be necessary to raise a Change Request to secure formal approval of the consequent changes (Sect. 5.6).

5.5 Work Breakdown Structure (WBS)

We have adopted the following definition of a Work Breakdown Structure (WBS): A formal and systematic way of defining and identifying what the component parts of a project are, breaking down the work to be planned, structuring, and integrating the project organisation and the control and information systems. Figure 5.1 shows an example of a high-level Work Breakdown Structure that shows the various levels of a typical WBS such as work package, activity, and task.

The WBS is a mechanism for splitting a large complex undertaking—the whole initiative/project—into smaller components, progressively reducing the scope and, complexity of each, down to a level at which individual tasks can be defined and costed.

The full breakdown gives the initiative owner/project manager confidence that the extent of the initiative/project has been correctly defined. In practice this level of detail may be more than is needed for 'monitoring and control' purposes. The individual functions may have lower level, more detailed schedules that "roll-up or feed" into the initiative owner's/project manager's schedule.

There are several different, but valid, ways in which to approach the WBS. The preferred approach is to base it on type of work. This avoids time or organisation-dependent structures, which can mask project requirements. It is important to focus on deliverables, not the contribution required from individual functions.

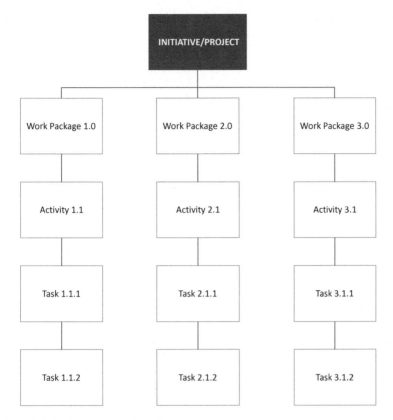

Fig. 5.1 High-level Work Breakdown Structure

A good WBS will have the following features:

- It gives a complete view of the initiative/project, including management and administrative tasks
- Each element appears only once, that is, there is no duplication
- At each level, every element is defined to a similar degree of detail (duration, effort, and so on)
- At a given level, the elements should be of the same type: this may be time, Departmental, functional, or category of work; types must not be mixed across the same level
- It should include any necessary approvals of work done.

The main definition of the WBS takes place at the Project Definition Workshop (PDW), led by the initiative owner/project manager (Sect. 5.1). This may include an informal 'brainstorming' session to arrive at a first cut WBS.

By adopting a systematic approach, the risk of leaving gaps or duplicating work is minimised. Even so, defining a WBS is not easy and initiative owners/project managers must develop expertise in this area. Completing the detailed breakdown may require additional information from functional experts and cross-functional discussions to identify everything that needs to be done, so the final WBS will probably not be completed at the PDW.

Often it will be possible to base the WBS on a previous similar work, but it is important to review every element: the time saved by replication must be weighed against the risk of not doing a full analysis.

> NOTE: The number of levels in a WBS depends on the scale and complexity of the initiative/project. As a rough guide, the duration of tasks at the lowest level should be at least 1 day and no longer than 10 days.

Producing the WBS identifies all the tasks that need to be done. The next step is to define these tasks and the logical relationships between them.

Defining Work Packages
Work packages are discrete packages of work, usually functional, that have an observable start and end date and include areas such as design, work or sign off process and communication.

Defining Activities
An activity represents a unit of work that is assignable to a single functional area. It has a planned start and end date, which spans the tasks that underlie. Activities contain tasks and deliverable milestones, once an activity is complete, the 'customer' or 'sponsor' should have something of value.

Defining Tasks
A task represents work at the lowest level. Usually tasks have resource (both labour and material), cost, duration and effort allocated to them. Once the tasks are known, their logical relationship can be established.

5.6   Change Control

Changes can occur in an initiative/project for any number of reasons, for example:

- Changes in Requirement due to altered business circumstances affecting time to market, scope, or way of working.
- Deviations from schedule due to slippage of one or more work-streams.
- Additional requirements that logically should be delivered in this initiative/project.
- "Scope creep". Good ideas that are included and should be captured.

The purpose of change control is to provide the initiative owner/project manager with a mechanism for obtaining the authority to adopt a new set of time, cost, and quality objectives. For this to happen, the change needs to be defined; evaluated for impact; communicated and agreed with all relevant parties; and is implementable via a clear action plan.

All changes to an initiative/project must be carefully managed so that their impact on the original schedule is clearly understood and any actions required to implement them are identified and incorporated into the initiative/project. Every initiative owner/project manager must maintain a formal record of what is under change control. This is normally visible in the documents, registers and paperwork which comprise the initiative/project management file.

The very nature of change control is that it is a means to control that which was not anticipated. Equally this document cannot anticipate all possibilities. The following are guidelines to aid the proper management and control of changes.

Scope
This change control procedure applies to all cross-functional initiatives/projects. It should not be used for managing change in relation to the following:

- Initiatives/projects that have a unitary structure, for example, there is no cross-functional element
- Live products/services/systems
- Business processes
- Service Level Agreements (SLA)
- Network configurations
- Documents not registered against an initiative/project
- New initiatives not formally approved by the organisation's Review Board (where one exists)

Checklist
Formal responsibilities are divided between the initiative/project sponsor, the initiative/project manager, and any line manager/supervisor involved, as described herein. Within each area the initiative owner/project manager appoints a line manager/supervisor who is the single point of contact in that area for processing change requests. The line manager/supervisor manages all aspects of the procedure within the function. This includes raising, chasing, championing, and communicating the change (Table 5.5).

Agree Change Acceptance Criteria for the Initiative/Project
The Initiative Owner/Project Manager must agree the basis of acceptance criteria for change requests with the Initiative/Project Sponsor. These criteria should set out how significant the proposed change needs to be before having to follow this process and the levels of delegated authority for approving change requests. These criteria provide a framework for the Change Control process. Each Change Request may

Table 5.5 Change control checklist

Change control checklist

Action	Responsible	Action	Tick if complete
Agree Change Acceptance Criteria for the Initiative/ Project	Project Sponsor	Project Manager	
Raise Change Request Form	Local Line Manager/ Supervisor	Local Line Manager/ Supervisor	
Local Impact Analysis	Local Line Manager/ Supervisor	Local team	
Register with Initiative Owner/ Project Manager	Local Line Manager/ Supervisor	Initiative Owner/ Project Manager	
Distribute Change	Initiative Owner/Project Manager	Local Line Manager/ Supervisor	
Impact Analysis	Line Managers/Supervisors appointed as single point of contact	All affected Line Managers/ Supervisors	
Overall Assessment of Impact Analyses	Initiative Owner/Project Manager	All affected Line Managers/ Supervisors	
Evaluate/Decide	Project Sponsor	Initiative Owner/ Project Manager	
Communicate Change	Initiative Owner/Project Manager	Initiative Owner/ Project Manager	
Implement Change	Initiative Owner/Project Manager	All	
Exceptions: Appeals; Retrospective Change control and Fast-Tracking	CEO/Director/Senior Manager	Project Manager/ Project Sponsor	

also need additional acceptance criteria to be defined and agreed before implementing this process.

Raising the Change Request Form

Any involved party can identify the need for a change. The course of action proposed by the change request will normally be designed to maintain the Time, Cost and Quality objectives as close to those existing before the change whilst accommodating the change itself.

The person wishing to raise a Change Request, having identified the requirement, notifies the local Line Manager/Supervisor, who has been appointed by the initiative owner/project manager as the single point of contact in that area for processing Change Requests. The change may be initiated by a party within or without the affected functional group. The Line Manager/Supervisor remains responsible for this stage regardless of source.

The change request is logged internally, and the form raised (Appendix Q). The change request must state clearly what is being changed, the justification and the action required. A change request may also identify possible ways of implementing the required change and evaluating the impact of each, before deciding which course of action to accept.

If at any stage the need for a change goes away or substantially alters, the Change Request may be withdrawn. Change Requests should be withdrawn only if the change is no longer needed or the requirements themselves change again before the change is approved. The raising Line Manager/Supervisor issues a memo to this effect and sends the Change Request Form to the initiative owner/project manager.

Local Impact Analysis
The Line Manager/Supervisor authorises the form and ensures that an impact analysis within his/her area is completed. This may be in two stages with an initial viability check but must be comprehensive before proceeding to the next stage. Having satisfactorily completed the local impact analysis, the Line Manager/Supervisor should then register the change with the initiative owner/project manager.

Register with Initiative Owner/Project Manager
The initiative owner/project manager maintains the master change record, the Initiative/Project Change Request Register (Appendix R). A favourable outcome of the internal function impact analysis results in discussion with the relevant initiative owner/project manager and other interested parties. The contents of the Change Request Form are updated. The initiative owner/project manager now owns the form although the processing may remain delegated with the Line Manager/Supervisor depending on the nature of the change. The change request is now registered on the Project Change Request Register (Appendix R).

Distributing the Change Request Form
Having registered the Change Request, the initiative owner/project manager distributes the Change Request Form, along with the internal Impact Analysis and any additional information, to all the other Line Managers/Supervisors appointed as central points of contact for change control, for impact analysis by the rest of the organisation. Each Line Manager/Supervisor circulates the Change Request Form within his/her area of responsibility.

Impact Analysis
All parties potentially affected by the change must have an opportunity to evaluate its impact. Where alternative solutions are available the optimum may be established at this time. The analysis should be quantitative and relate to current baselines as defined in any business case/PDD and other documentation.

Functional responses are mandatory or discretionary, according to a list maintained by the initiative owner/project manager. **Those functions whose response is mandatory must provide an Impact Analysis, even if there is no impact.** Appendix T summarises the Impact Analysis.

Overall Assessment of Impact Analyses

Each Line Manager/Supervisor, appointed as central point of contact, obtains, and consolidates the Functional Impact Analysis and returns it to the initiative owner/ project manager. The initiative owner/project manager is responsible for tracking the overall progress of the Impact Analysis. Individual Line Managers/Supervisors are responsible for tracking the progress of the Impact Analysis within his or her own functional area. If no response is received within the required time frame, the initiative owner/project manager will publish, 'no impact'. If the area concerned is on the mandatory response list, then the issue should be escalated by the initiative owner/project manager to a Senior Manager/Executive or Director, who will determine if the risk of missing an impact is outweighed by the benefit of reaching a prompt decision. The appeals process offers a safety net if the wrong decision is reached.

The Initiative Owner Project Manager must consolidate the individual Impact Analyses. When all the functional Impact Analyses have been completed and returned, the initiative owner/project manager prepares and evaluates a consolidated Impact Analysis. If there is not enough information for making an appropriate decision, then he/she will ask relevant functions to undertake further analysis.

Evaluating/Deciding on the Change Request

The initiative sponsor/project owner decides whether the Change Request is REJECTED or ACCEPTED by comparing the consolidated Impact Analysis against criteria established when the Change Request was raised. The initiative sponsor/ project owner must decide based on a consolidated impact analysis. The raising Line Manager/Supervisor may be called on to assist in the resolution of issues arising out of contentious or complex Change Requests.

No individual area can veto a change based on their own views if the overall impact is acceptable to the initiative sponsor/project owner. Equally, if the consolidated Impact Analysis is not acceptable, no one party can force the change through. If the overall impact significantly changes the Business Case/PDD, the initiative sponsor/project owner may not have the authority to agree the change without reference to the relevant approval body.

If a Change Request remains open for more than a month, its continuing relevance should be reviewed. If still required but no acceptable solution can be found the reason should be established. It may be due to:

- Departmental priority. (Initiative Sponsor/Project Owner to resolve)
- Budget restriction. (Initiative Sponsor/Project Owner to resolve)
- Technical Difficulty. (Initiative Owner/Project Manager to resolve)
- Coming Events. (Initiative Sponsor/Project Owner to resolve)

If resolution is not attained, then the change must be abandoned or deferred to another project at the discretion of the Initiative Sponsor/Project Owner.

The Initiative Owner/Project Manager and Initiative Sponsor/Project Owner both must sign the Change Request Form to confirm the decision to accept or reject the change.

Note that even if a change proposal is rejected, the reason for its being originated probably still exists. It may be necessary to take alternative action to ensure that the project continues in an acceptable fashion. This may result in another change request or its inclusion in an alternative project. Action consequent upon rejection of a change proposal is the responsibility of the Initiative Sponsor/Project Owner.

Communication of Change Requests
The initiative owner/project manager communicates the decision on the Change Request to the Line Managers/Supervisors and other affected parties—for example within initiatives/projects on whom there is a dependency. This memo summarises the basis of the decision and the actions required to implement the change.

The initiative owner/project manager files the signed Change Request and a copy of the consolidated Impact Analysis. This constitutes the formal record of the change and is liable to audit.

Implementing Agreed Changes
The Initiative Owner/Project Manager must ensure that all actions required to implement or to effect the change are incorporated into the initiative/project plans and that controlled documents are updated. There may also be consequent changes in the status of initiative/project risks. The initiative owner/project manager is responsible for managing the implementation of the agreed change. Under the direction of the initiative owner/project manager, each function incorporates the actions required to implement the change into their plans and updates any documentation under their control. The implementation of the agreed changes will be monitored through standard initiative/project review processes.

Exceptions: Appeals; Retrospective Change Control and Fast-Tracking
Any relevant party who does not agree with the decision can appeal to the initiative sponsor/project owner. We suggest appointing a senior business manager to review the decision, and if necessary, consulting relevant parties who have contributed to the Impact Analysis. If the original decision is changed, a further memo must be issued to the initiative owner/project manager to update relevant records accordingly, advise relevant parties of the revised decision and update initiative/project records accordingly.

On occasion a change is implemented without change control procedure being applied. This is not acceptable as routine practice regardless of urgency. Action should be taken to avoid repetition. However appropriate elements of this procedure should be applied to retain a complete record in such cases. Those cases where an uncontrolled change would not have been approved, had the procedure been followed, are interesting. The uncontrolled change should only be reversed if to do so offers overall benefit from the current initiative/project status.

A minimum period of 10 working days likely to be required to complete the change control process. The initiative owner/project manager may set a faster time scale, where justified, but should bear in mind that the basic procedure must be followed and that it will be necessary to walk the request personally or convene a meeting of all key parties and that an impact analysis is mandatory. The initiative sponsor/project owner still must decide on the acceptability. The key players must include:

- Raiser
- Initiative Owner/Project Manager
- Initiative Sponsor/Project Owner
- Impact analysers from all functions
- Other interested parties (as identified by the Initiative Owner/Project Manager).

The aim of the meeting is to get all the relevant parties together to address the impact of the change and the issues surrounding it, with the objective of deciding and agreeing actions to implement it. Therefore, all parties attending the meeting should have the necessary decision-making authority. Meeting details must be formally recorded and signed by all participants and must include all parameters to complete the change definition.

The change request is then circulated to all interested parties as complete and closed in the normal way. Alternatively, the above group may be consulted on a 'one by one basis' by the initiative owner/project manager 'walking round'. Signed agreement to the proposal is required from each party. In either case a rapid and documented decision is achieved. Documentation is then distributed as normal.

Post-Change Review
As part of an initiative's/project's 'closedown', or earlier in the life cycle, it may be necessary to review the actual impact of implementing the agreed change. The appropriate form (Appendix S) should be used for this purpose.

5.7   Scheduling

Validating the Schedule
The baselined, costed schedule tells the initiative owner/project manager whether the initiative/project can meet the target milestones and costs, as set out in the signed-off Business Case/PDD. If the calculated estimates are outside the tolerances agreed

with the initiative sponsor/project owner, the initiative owner/project manager must decide whether to attempt to create a new schedule, or to seek to modify the initiative/project definition (or design). The schedule can be modified in several ways; add more resource, modify logic, or shorten durations.

Resource Scheduling and Constraints

The assumptions made in calculating the schedule represent an 'ideal' of unlimited experience and resource with no external constraints. In the real world, initiatives/projects will have to share resources, or there may be a limitation on the availability of a given skill, so it will not always be possible to have a particular person or group exactly when needed. Also, external factors (such as delivery dates of equipment or the availability of test platforms) may affect the 'ideal' schedule.

The initiative owner/project manager must now recalculate the schedule based on actual resource availability. Planned availability should consider holidays, sickness, overheads, and training. A further refinement is 'resource smoothing' to avoid uneven work patterns.

If the initiative/project is cross-functional the resource assignments must be negotiated with each function, and Line Managers/Supervisors must agree the assignments. Once agreed this is a commitment, which cannot be revoked without the initiative owner's/project manager's consent. The schedule now has a named individual responsible for each task and is ready for formal approval.

Functional Resource Planning

To be able to confirm that resources are available to carry out the schedule at the required time, each function must maintain a functional resource plan. This is an integrated schedule showing all tasks being done by people from the function across all initiatives/projects. To demonstrate that the functional schedules are robust, it may be necessary to include tasks at a greater level of detail than that agreed in the cross-functional schedule for a given initiative/project.

It is the functional representative's responsibility to:

- Determine what to include in the functional schedule
- Ensure that overall, functional resource schedules remain valid and stable
- Establish appropriate mechanisms for providing necessary progress information as agreed

Approving the Schedule

Each function signs up to the schedule, agreeing that they have the nominated people available at the time the initiative/project requires them. Sign-off also implies that external constraints, for example test-bed availability, have been addressed.

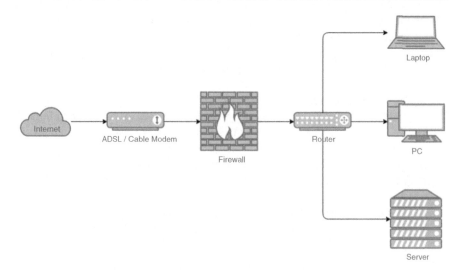

Fig. 5.2 Sample Network Diagram

Baselining the Schedule
Once an initiative/project has secured approval, the functions proceed to allocate and direct their resources to undertake the tasks agreed and the schedule is 'baselined', becoming subject to change control (Sect. 5.6).

The objective of baselining the schedule is to ensure that the assumptions and estimates used (normally during Gate 2 and 3) are still valid and to provide a benchmark against which to measure progress. This ensures that the initiative/project team and each functional group involved with the initiative/project understand fully what is being delivered and how much it costs.

Presenting the Schedule
There are several ways in which an initiative/project schedule can be presented. Initiative/project planning tools normally offer a selection of standard fonts or templates which can be modified to suit a particular initiative's/project's requirements. The common formats are:

- Network diagram (or PERT chart).
- Gantt chart
- Milestone list
- Checklist or countdown plan

Network Diagram
A network diagram is a representation of the schedule showing the logical links between the tasks. The WBS gives no information about the order of play or the

dependencies between tasks. Some tasks follow on from others, some can be done in parallel. It is therefore necessary to determine the logical order in which the tasks must be done. This requires input from all contributing functions and the result is a Network Diagram (sometimes known as a PERT Chart), showing all the tasks and how they are related in time (Fig. 5.2).

Network Diagrams can be done manually or by using a project management tool. It is easier in the initial stages to define the dependencies of the initiative/project manually.

It is important that all functions agree that the Network Diagram is correct, as it defines inter-functional dependencies.

Initially the diagram will need to include all the tasks identified in the WBS. It may be possible later to aggregate tasks, if appropriate (for example, where they are all carried out within one function as part of one work package, where the elapsed times are relatively short and where there are no significant deliverables or events in the middle of them).

Once the network diagram has been agreed it will generally be necessary to put the plan on a project management tool so that the schedule and, later, the impact of changes can be automatically calculated.

Gantt Chart
A Gantt chart is a way of showing the tasks in a schedule, as a series of horizontal bars along a time scale. Normally these will be organised by people or work groups (Fig. 5.3).

Milestone List
A milestone list is a list of controlled milestones showing the owner, the target delivery date, and the current planned date (Fig. 5.3).

Key milestones relating to principal deliverables and work package dates will be identified early on, probably during the Project Definition Workshop (Sect. 5.1).

Key milestones mark the completion of specific deliverables and should be selected so that they are evenly spread over the lifetime of the initiative/project and amongst the contributing functions. Before the schedule is approved the initiative owner/project manager must agree the key milestones with the initiative/project team or functional representatives.

From the network diagram it will be possible to identify other milestones which will help in monitoring and controlling the initiative/project. A provisional target date should be assigned to each milestone; it might need to be revised when the task durations are estimated, and the schedule is baselined (Table 5.6).

Strategic Plan for New Business

#	Name	Duration	Start	Finish
1	Self-Assessment	23,0 d	03.01.2011	05.01.2011
2	Define business vision	1,0 d	03.01.2011	03.01.2011
3	Identify available skills, information and support	1,0 d	04.01.2011	04.01.2011
4	Decide whether to proceed	1,0 d	05.01.2011	05.01.2011
5	Define the Opportunity	10,0 d	06.01.2011	19.01.2011
6	Research the market & competition	1,0 d	06.01.2011	06.01.2011
7	Interview owners of similar businesses	5,0 d	07.01.2011	13.01.2011
8	Identify needed resources	2,0 d	14.01.2011	17.01.2011
9	Identify operating cost elements	2,0 d	18.01.2011	19.01.2011
10	Evaluate Business Approach	4,0 d	20.01.2011	25.01.2011
11	Define new entity requirements	1,0 d	20.01.2011	20.01.2011
12	Identify on-going business purchase opportunities	1,0 d	21.01.2011	21.01.2011
13	Research franchise possibilities	1,0 d	24.01.2011	24.01.2011
14	Summarize business approach	1,0 d	25.01.2011	25.01.2011
15	Evaluate Potential Risks and Rewards	7,0 d	21.01.2011	31.01.2011
16	Assess market size and stability	2,0 d	21.01.2011	24.01.2011
17	Estimate the competition	1,0 d	25.01.2011	25.01.2011
18	Assess needed resource availability	2,0 d	26.01.2011	27.01.2011
19	Evaluate realistic initial market share	1,0 d	28.01.2011	28.01.2011
20	Determine financial requirements	2,0 d	26.01.2011	27.01.2011
21	Review personal suitability	1,0 d	28.01.2011	28.01.2011
22	Evaluate initial profitability	1,0 d	31.01.2011	31.01.2011
23	Review and modify the strategic plan	2,0 d	01.02.2011	02.02.2011
24	Confirm decision to proceed		03.02.2011	

Fig. 5.3 Sample Gantt chart

Table 5.6 Example milestone report

Key milestone report					
Initiative/Project	XYZ	Ref.	123	Date	31/8/21
Owner	**Milestone**	**Target**	**Planned**	**Actual**	
Customer	Requirements fully signed off	21/1/98	21/1/98	28/1/98	
Initiative Owner/ Project Manager	Initiative/Project Team formed	9/2/98	16/2/98	16/2/98	
Network Engineering	Process Changes Agreed	31/7/21	15/8/21	31/8/21	
Software Development Team	Code released for independent testing	10/7/21	21/7/21	8/8/21	

Planning Tools
We suggest the following use of different planning tools:

- Micro Planner for Windows, Microsoft Project, Project Manager Workbench
- Online solutions such as Gantter, Smartsheet
- Or any open Access Alternative Options

Addendum: An Introduction to the Concepts of Agile and Scrum

6

6.1 Background

We consider it worthwhile to spend a little bit of time explaining to the reader how the concepts of Agile and SCRUM can be applied in Innovation Scorecard measurement environments. Where do these concepts emanate from? The idea of 'agile business' (doing things fast and dexterous) was developed in 2001 by a group of like-minded business professionals, in a totally relaxing environment, united to create an alternative to the less flexible 'waterfall model' (cascading) in, use at that time, in software development. This model was not able to respond quickly to changes and constant changing requirements often driven by customer needs, business needs, or both. This group created a document known as the 'agile manifest'. This manifest contained what they considered to be the most important principles that needed to be in place to make this approach work in all kinds of business environments.

1. Our highest priority is to satisfy the customer through early and continuous delivery of valuable software.
2. Welcome changing requirements, even late in development. Agile processes harness change for the customer's competitive advantage.
3. Deliver working software frequently, from a couple of weeks to a couple of months, with a preference to the shorter timescale.
4. Business managers and developers must work together daily throughout the project.
5. Build projects around motivated individuals. Give them the environment and support their needs and trust them to get the job done.
6. The most efficient and effective method of conveying information to and within a development team is face-to-face conversation.
7. Working software is the primary measure of progress.
8. Agile processes promote sustainable development. The sponsors, developers, and users should be able to maintain a constant pace indefinitely.

O. Zizlavsky, E. Fisher, *Innovation Scorecard*, Management for Professionals,
https://doi.org/10.1007/978-3-030-82688-8_6

9. Continuous attention to technical excellence and good design enhances agility.
10. Simplicity—the art of maximising the amount of work not done—is essential.
11. The best architectures, requirements, and designs emerge from self-organising teams.
12. At regular intervals, the team reflects on how to become more effective, then tunes and adjusts its behaviour accordingly (https://agilemanifesto.org/principles.html).

Beck et al. (2001), based on these 12 principles of agile software development, define the four values that need to be followed to make this work successfully as:

- Individuals and interactions over processes and tools
- Working software over comprehensive documentation
- Customer collaboration over contract negotiation
- Responding to change over following a plan

6.2   Agile Methodology

According to the Association for Project Management, 'iterative life cycles are composed of several iterations allowing the deployment of initial capability, followed by successive deliveries of further value' (APM, 2019, p. 20). This allows for different development steps to be performed in parallel. Iterative life cycles are repetitive (phases are repeated time and time again before proceeding to the next one). This allows for objectives to be achieved by making sure that any learning and discovery are incorporated in the process. This approach has distinct advantages. A high emphasis is place on team collaboration and encourages teams to be highly creative. It deals with and manages the concepts of change, innovation and introducing new domains into any business environment. Agile methods often apply a so-called 'time boxing' approach. It simply means that a fixed time is blocked out in, for example, the initiative/project calendar. To deliver on time and to cost, the initiative/project owner needs to focus their attention on adjusting the scope and quality to achieve the set time and cost constraints. This approach also benefits from engaging users more in the process and this leads to earlier validation of, for example, proof of concepts. Earlier returns on planned benefits can also be achieved sooner.

Gradually, the agile approach proved successful not only in the development of software, but overall, in product or solution development and has become very popular in other sectors. It has now also started to play a key role in areas such as finance, telecommunications, marketing, and human resource management (HRM), according to Ashmore and Runyan (2014).

Further Reading: Agile Institute of Professional Studies, www.agileips.com

6.3   Scrum

It appears that the software development term Scrum originated from a research article published by Hirotaka Takeuchi and Ijujiro Nonaka, in the January 1986 issue of Harvard Business Review. The term Scrum was borrowed from the game of Rugby where Scrum refers to a formation of players (the most effective and efficient way of getting the ball from point A to point B). In management terms, according to Myslin (2016), Scrum is a comprehensive managerial methodology that is made up of a complete solution how teamwork should be organised to get the most out of people and to deliver work faster. Scrum was developed to support managing development processes in the most efficient way. This method is well-known for not containing specific tools, technologies and procedures relating to how scrum developers should use it. Instead, it shows how the whole team should work together and how they should communicate to deliver work optimally. Scrum is based on the knowledge that development brings with it a lot of unpredictable events and thus becomes complex. It is a largely managerial methodology which focuses on monitoring and addressing all obstacles that could lead to successful software development.

6.3.1   Typical Scrum Framework

To understand Scrum, it is necessary to understand the roles of people within its framework/processes and to gain a good understanding of the individual parts that make up the scrum framework and its associated processes (Fig. 6.1). The whole point of Scrum is to do whatever it takes to get the job done successfully. A typical Scrum team is made up of three people with clearly and specifically defined roles and

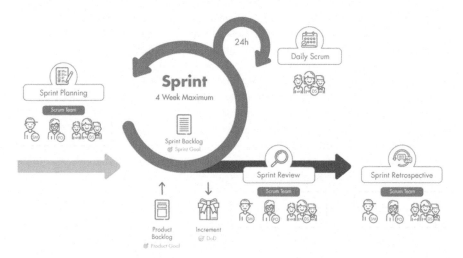

Fig. 6.1 Scrum framework (Rodríguez, 2021)

responsibilities: a product owner, Scrum master and the development team. Scrum teams are cross-functional and are therefore made up of a variety of people who hold different roles in the organisation such as developers, testers, designers, or operational support staff. People performing these roles work closely together to ensure a smooth flow of information and quickly solve problems (Šochova & Kunce, 2014).

6.3.2 The Scrum Process

The scrum team executes on the product owner's vision. They decide what gets built and the order in which it gets built. The product owner represents the best interest of the end user and ensures that what the customer wants or expects will be delivered. The product owner has the final veto as far as the end delivery is concerned. The product owner is responsible for preparing, for example, any product backlog, a list of tasks and the requirements of what the final product should look like. The product owner is the only point of contact for all questions relating to product requirements. At this stage, it is necessary for the product owner to prioritise the work ensuring tasks are performed in the right sequence. This is generally referred to, within software development, as 'backlog'.

Sprint Planning Meetings form an essential part of the Scrum process or framework. Product Owner, the team and Scrum master meet at regular intervals to sort out and agree what the main priority tasks are and to select which of these priority tasks will be actioned to go forward to the next stage. The outputs from Sprint Planning effectively become the sprint backlog referred to earlier, in effect describing the requirements the end customer expects (Sutherland, 2014).

The next stage is a sprint that represents a predetermined timeframe in which a team must complete task sets from a specific backlog. The length of time depends on the needs of the team, but the duration is typically between 1 and 2 weeks. Sprints are vital to the successful delivery of the intended outputs. It is for this reason that the main emphasis is placed on team empowerment. The team knows what the best solutions are, for example, how to make things work. They are given the autonomy to do whatever it takes to get the job done. Team size usually ranges from five to nine team members. So-called daily Scrum team meetings are held to share and discuss progress made. This is important. It allows the team to take immediate corrective action to fix any problems, thus avoiding any lengthy and unnecessary delays. Another valuable contribution these sprints make to the whole process: they assist to produce what are considered potentially shippable products (products ready for distribution to the customer). The product owner has the final say as to whether these products have all the features the customer asked for and whether set and agreed quality standards have been achieved.

Each sprint ends with a review. This is sometimes called a 'lessons learned' review and in agile projects this is referred to as a "Mini Post Implementation Review". The team reviews the outputs with the product owner so they can identify potential areas for improvement for the next sprint. This process is repeated until the final product has been created to the desired and expected quality standards.

The whole process is overseen by the Scrum master who is responsible for the smooth running of the process, for dissolving obstacles/issues that affect productivity/quality and for organising and facilitating critical follow-up meetings (Myslín, 2016).

Further reading: www.scrum-institute.org
   Clayton, S.J. (2021). An Agile Approach to Change Management. Harvard Business Review. https://hbr.org/2021/01/an-agile-approach-to-change-management
   Lines, M. (2021). Celebrating 20 Years of the Agile Manifesto. PMI Blog. https://community.pmi.org/t5/the-official-pmi-blog/celebrating-20-years-of-the-agile-manifesto/ba-p/242

6.4   Innovation Scorecard and Agile Working Environment

You may ask why the concept of agile is relevant to the management of Innovation Scorecard initiatives/projects in work environments?

A system that is fast and flexible at the same time and a system that can respond to changes swiftly adds value to users of an Agile approach. Focusing on results rather than adhering to a rigid and strict process is of paramount importance to the successful delivery of so-called Agile projects or work. Two of the many advantages of Agile/Scrum per se are their inherent flexibility and their ability to react fast to changes. This approach is dynamic and provides quick access to solutions within software development environments, for example. The Innovation Scorecard, just like Agile, applies a similar 'logical steps' implementation process. We suggest that merging the two concepts is vital for success. Combined, the two concepts of Agile and Innovation Scorecard produce a unified measurement system. The advantage of this approach is not always self-evident. Agile work environments, by definition, can be 'chaotic' at the best of times. The Innovation Scorecard can bring 'order' to this undesirable situation. Applying this combined approach appropriately, ensures that the concept of agile (doing something righteous and fast) is not compromised. We suggest that this approach is dynamic and provides quick access to solutions, especially in software development environments. At first glance it appears that the immeasurable can be measured. A combination of a dynamic change process such as Innovation Scorecard and a significant project management control system such as Agile can achieve things that are greater than their combined parts. You should consider setting up a management control 'role' within your team (or ensure that support is available) to collect, analyse and evaluate relevant 'operational data', at the right quantity, right quality, and right time to aid decision making.

References

Ashmore, S., & Runyan, K. (2014). *Introduction to agile methods*. Addison-Wesley Professional.
Association for Project Management. (2019). *Body of knowledge* (7th ed.). Association for Project Management (APM).
Beck, K., et al. (2001). *Agile manifesto* [on-line]. https://agilemanifesto.org/
Myslin, J. (2016). *Scrum: průvodce agilním vývojem softwaru*. Computer Press.
Rodríguez, M. (2021). *The past, present, and future of Scrum* [on-line]. https://netmind.net/en/the-past-present-and-future-of-scrum/
Šochova, Z., & Kunce, E. (2014). *Agilní metody řízení projektů*. Computer Press.
Sutherland, J. (2014). *Scrum: The art of doing twice the work in half the time*,. Crown.

Further Reading

Association for Project Management. (2016). *Directing agile change*. Association for Project Management (APM).
Drucker, P. F. (2009). *Innovation and entrepreneurship*. Harper Business.
Haughey, D. (2011). *BOSCARD: Terms of reference. Project Smart*. [on-line]. https://www.projectsmart.co.uk/boscard.php
Henley, J. (2015). *Scrum: How to leverage user stories for better requirements definition (Scrum Series Book 2)*. Axellerata Publishing.
Takeuchi, H., & Nonaka, I. (1986). The new product development game. *Harvard Business Review, 64*(1).

Part II
Practice

Case Study 1: Red Hat Enterprise Linux (RHEL) Atomic Host

7.1 Background

Red Hat® Enterprise Linux (RHEL) Atomic Host is a secure, lightweight, and minimal-footprint operating system optimized to run Linux containers. A member of the Red Hat Enterprise Linux (RHEL) family, its Atomic Host system couples the flexible, modular capabilities of Linux containers with the reliability and security of RHEL in a reduced footprint, to decrease the attack surface and provide only the packages needed to power hardware and run containers. Red Hat's vision for containerized application delivery on an open hybrid cloud infrastructure is comprehensive, including portability across bare metal systems, virtual machines, and private/public clouds. By choosing Red Hat Enterprise Linux Atomic Host, customers can take advantage of the fast pace of innovation from open-source community projects like the Docker project and Project Atomic while maintaining a stable platform for production deployment. Customers can concentrate on customizing and developing containerized applications while Red Hat maintains the underlying Linux platform on which these depend. Atomic Host was chosen to act as the pilot study for introducing the concept of Innovation Scorecard to measure the success of deployed modus operandi improvements within this agile software development project.

The main goal of this case study is to report and discuss how the research team adopted and adapted the chosen Innovation Scorecard system to ensure it was fit for the intended purpose for roll out within Red Hat's Agile project management work environment. This includes, and is not limited to, describing the details of prevailing local current process conditions, the design of the system, its implementation and a verification framework that was applied for the introduction of this process improvement system.

© The Author(s), under exclusive license to Springer Nature Switzerland AG 2021   81
O. Zizlavsky, E. Fisher, *Innovation Scorecard*, Management for Professionals,
https://doi.org/10.1007/978-3-030-82688-8_7

7.2   Current Atomic Host Process

To understand how the applied Atomic Host process (Fig. 7.1) that is applied within Red Hat works, it is necessary for the reader to familiarise themselves with the various stages involved in this process. The following is a brief description of how this process works and how it is practically applied in the real world.

Each updating batch is planned to be developed, tested, and released over a period of 6 weeks (Fig. 7.1). Work starts with a **planning phase** that typically lasts for 10 days. It is based on the outputs from Sprint Planning Meeting(s). These meetings are attended by the Product Owner, Product Manager, and team members. The Product Owner presents a set of features he/she would like to see completed in the sprint (the 'what'). The team then determines the tasks needed to implement these features (the 'how'). Work estimates are reviewed to see if the team has the time to complete all the features requested in the sprint. If yes, the team commits to the sprint. If no, the lower priority features go back into the product backlog until the workload for the sprint is small enough to obtain the team's commitment.

The **development phase** follows. This includes individual sprints and usually lasts for 30 days. Development work is managed and completed applying an agile work approach known as Scrum. It consists of two sprints, and each takes 2 weeks. It can also include a third optional sprint if it is needed (this decision is made during the planning phase). In the development phase, everything is based on, for example, any backlog from the preceding planning phase. At the end of the development phase, there is a development freeze. It means that the development is closed for any further work to be undertaken. Developers confirm and provide relevant information that all packages are ready and available to proceed to the testing stage.

The **testing phase** consists of two steps. First, Early Build and Testing is performed. The building process takes 3 days. Its purpose is to put together all components and associated packages. Early testing follows which takes 10 days. If there is a delay in the building process such as 3+2 days, then Early testing must be shortened such as 10 days minus 2 days. Some lateness in Early testing is not a big issue. Early testing is deployed to identify any issues/problems as early as possible and then take corrective action. Any delay in this phase does not have a big impact on the General Availability (GA) of updated batches. When early testing is completed successfully, Final build and testing (also referred to as launch) follows. The process of this launch is the same as Early build and testing, for example, to build final packages and appropriate containers and then test them. Time allowed for the Final build is 3 days. Testing takes 5 days. If passed successfully then an Atomic Host is created. Any issues during the launch phase have a huge impact on the final GA. An agreement is in place that GA cannot slip by more than 3 days.

7.2.1   Atomic Host Build Process

The build process includes two identical steps: Early and Final (launch) Build. The whole process is initiated by the Czech Republic-based Programme Manager. He

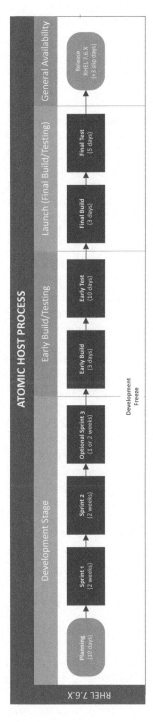

Fig. 7.1 Atomic Host process

instructs the RHEL release team, located in the US, to create so-called 'compose' and other required 'images' required for the early, for example, code build. Once these images have been produced, they are tested by a Quality Engineer (QE), located in the US, who will conduct appropriate test automation activities within a developed test infrastructure, including the execution of test cases on this developed infrastructure. If the created images are not correct or acceptable, they must be returned to RHEL Release Team. If they are verified and accepted, they will be submitted to complete a process known as 'extra compose' which involves running these images on a test environment to verify their acceptance for roll-out and integration. The 'extra compose' work is completed in the Czech Republic. Once re-testing has been completed, roll-out can commence via so-called 'containers' at global level. The build process is now complete and the Atomic Compose is created.

The Build Process itself (Fig. 7.2) has **two main challenges**. Location appears to be a major concern due to the different time zones involved. Overall, the process starts in the Czech Republic and is triggered by the Program Manager, with the release team located in the United States. As a result, the team starts preparation work (compose and images) minus 6 or 7 h behind Czech time. The verification by the Quality Engineer (QE) is also conducted in the US. Then some activities that follow are completed in the Czech Republic, at global and/or US level. Working in different time zones causes undesirable delays. Teams need to wait until working hours commence in countries other than their own. There are dependencies between working activities in different countries (sequential). This causes some repetitive manual work being done during periods of time overlaps. This causes frustration and appears to demotivate team members in various locations. It also reduces team members' time to be creative and proactive. The second area is the flow of Communication. The person mainly affected by this is the Program Manager. Over 40% of his time is spent communicating effectively with the various parties involved in the project. This is exacerbated by the need to communicate with team members who work in the different time zones mentioned earlier. The following areas that form part of the build process, have been identified by Red Hat senior management to carry high risks. These risks need to be managed by the Red Hat project manager. The identified risks form part of the build process:

- Quality Engineer (QE)
- Extra Compose
- **Container Rebuild Process**
- Atomic Host Compose

7.2.2 Container Rebuild Process Innovation

The initial pilot case study contained within this Red Hat project focuses on a 'container rebuild' initiative within Red Hat in support of a required process innovation automation tool, to provide support in terms of information, to provide metrics to measure the success of the innovations and to show impact/improvements

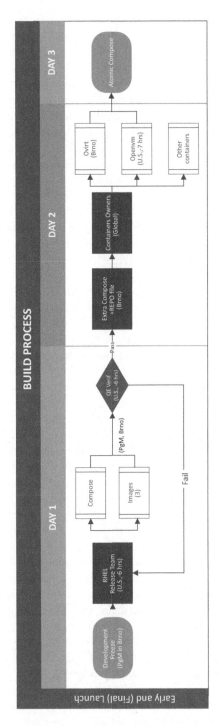

Fig. 7.2 Atomic Host build process

of the automation system. The whole process starts when the release engineering team creates 'compose and base' images within a development platform known as 'Docker' (www.docker.com). This platform contains all common configurations based on latest available packages. Docker is a platform specifically suitable for software developers so they can find and share container images with their team and for the benefit of the so-called 'Docker Community'. It appears that the Docker platform is the preferred choice for a tool that builds and shares containerised applications and microservices with the community of practice. Building and deploying new applications is faster with containers. Docker containers combine software and its dependencies in a single standardised unit for software development. This unit includes everything that is required to run the software successfully: a code, runtime system tools and libraries. This approach guarantees that applications will always run the same. It makes collaboration between developers as simple as sharing a container image. As soon as this activity has been completed, the details are handed over to the Quality Engineering (QE) team who will apply some engineering best practices to different parts of the software development process, thus increasing the quality of the overall product. In general, quality engineers are familiar with security testing and performance testing and are generally aware of Continuous Integration/Continuous Delivery (CI/CD) techniques. After the QE team have approved to proceed in principle, this process can continue to another area within the overall software development process known as 'layered container image'. Associated follow-on development phases are completed within 24 h. Time scales are very short to complete the whole development process as quickly as possible. Should any issues arise during this stage, the previous process of 'composing and base image' is repeated and re-tests will be conducted to fix any issues. The release team will inform the Program Manager in charge of this initiative once this work has been completed successfully. This includes details of the created compose Uniform Resource Locator (URL, referring to the location of a resource on a computer network) and what the name is of the base image file (IMG). The IMG format is usually applied to distribute programmes such as operating systems or applications. These files are essential for making and storing backup copies of software programmes just in case original files might get lost. This is the appropriate time for the Program Manager to advise relevant parties of what activities they need to complete next. Rebuild developers can commence their tasks once the earlier referred to 'Docker-file' has been updated by the relevant team. It is now possible to commence the actual build process. When the build process has been successfully completed, the owner reviews the Errata Updates which are released within Red Hat in three categories or types: security updates, bug fix updates and enhancement updates. Each of these updates is made up of a summary of what the actual problem is, how this can be resolved and what RPM (.rpm file format) packages need to be deployed to fix the identified problems. RPM Package Manager is a free and open-source package management system initially intended for use within Red Hat's Linux distributions. The completion of these sequentially dependent activities (Fig. 7.3) marks the end of this project phase. One of the most important phases in software development follows: end to end (E2E) and user acceptance testing (UAT).

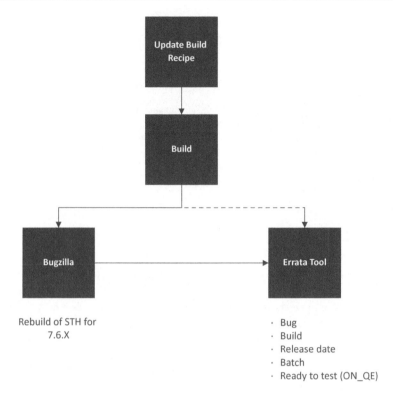

Fig. 7.3 Update build recipe

Once all testing is completed successfully, including unit, integration and user acceptance testing, and the release of the new build has been approved by the development team, the new and updated container image is uploaded to the public repository ready to be accessed by customers.

7.3   Objectives

The primary objective is to improve the 'Container Rebuild' process. This can be achieved by introducing innovative ways of working such as a new automation process (Table 7.1) so that repetitive manual work, currently carried out by the container image owners within RHEL's Atomic Host system, can be eliminated. In this context, 'bot' is defined as a program designed to automate tasks. A bot is a kind of software robot. The bot can carry out simple, repetitive, and routine tasks and perform these much faster than a human being could. This explains why the use of bots in software development has become so popular. In addition, 'Dist' stands for 'distributable' and it refers to a directory where files will be stored that can be directly used by others without the need to compile or minify the source code that is

Table 7.1 Manual and automation workflow comparison

No automation	Automation
• Owner makes changes. They do not receive any response about associated potential breakages/problems as part of this process. • Programme Manager sends out email to request new build. • Owner must update all Docker file versions. • Owner creates new Bugzilla. • Owner creates new erratum. • Owner creates new image. • Owner might test the image manually. • Owner attaches new image to erratum. • Owner switches the erratum to ON_QE.	• Bot runs a scratch build, immediate feedback loop secured. • Bot scans Docker file for error. • Docker file versions template created. • Owner merges changes. • Bot syncs changes to dist-git. • Bot makes a production build. • Bot creates new Bugzilla, erratum, attaches production build and switches the erratum.

being reused. 'Git' is a distributed version-control system for tracking changes in source code during software development. It is designed for coordinating work among programming team members, but it can equally be used to track changes in various file sets. As a direct result of the planned automation work, the Container Rebuild process will be shortened thus providing Red Hat team members with more time to focus their attention on fixing, for example, customers' problems more proactively and faster, becoming more creative and creating opportunities to take on board additional work. The automation process is expected to respond much more positively and proactively to operational failure situations. Should this occur, the new system will automatically, without any need for human intervention, return to the beginning of the process and resolve any issues.

Another important and essential objective of the Atomic Host project is to improve the current Red Hat release engineering processes that deal with the development and collection of source codes and putting these together in a single assembly. These are then installed into finished products or alternative software development components. In essence, release engineering is about building fast and reliable pipelines so that these source codes can be transformed into viable products so that these products have the capability of working successfully. Red Hat's automation team will be engaged in this change management initiative. This is vital to the successful rollout of the new work approach otherwise known as change or innovation management.

It is imperative that all members of the container team are fully conversant with the container build process and understand what their individual roles are within this process. Team members also need to be proactive in their outlooks and flexible as far as innovation is concerned. Innovation is about change and this is not necessarily something every person is comfortable with. Team leaders need to be aware of people's dispositions as this knowledge can make the difference between a success-ful innovation rollout or change failure. The Atomic Host approach adopts an approach that is based on avoiding confusion as far as good and effective communications are concerned, using both words and numerical presentations. This is essential for being successful. All those engaged in the Atomic Host process are provided with clear and concise information, so they fully understand what the subject matter is, for example, for discussion. Clear descriptions and explanations are provided to describe, for example, what the purpose is of a new approach, what a tool is there for to help the team members or a change in how something will be done differently from now on. It is clear to all team members who the owner is for each relevant piece of work or agreed action points, usually assigned during regular review or planning meetings.

Adopted Critical Success Factors (CSFs), Key Performance Indicators (KPIs) and set project goals are clearly defined, are expressed in both words and numbers, with clear target completion values set that are meaningful, achievable, and challenging. This fits in with the principles of the adopted Innovation Scorecard system applied to develop, deliver, and launch the Atomic Host initiative (and other associated projects) successfully and within customer expectations. The initial intention is to set challenging target values to stretch the Atomic Host team but without being unrealistic. The iScorecard Team considers that the so-called 'traffic light or Red Amber Green (RAG) system' for progress reporting, for example, in project management, is not considered suitable for the Atomic Host project. This type of reporting system is usually applied in non-agile projects due to the inherent nature of what 'agile' stands for (quick, swift, doing things dexterous, skilful), with the focus being on delivering and not getting side-tracked by anything that hinders the delivery. This approach is thought to be a new approach for use in Red Hat, and as such, for the people working in Red Hat. It requires a tactful and at the same time forceful change management approach that overall helps to introduce a new 'way of working' in areas of agile software development within Red Hat. As a direct result, the iScorecard Team considers that the adoption of simple and yet effective status and dashboard reporting systems is more appropriate. This includes but is not limited to regular progress reporting in areas such as last month achievements, planned activities for the next month, issues and risks and milestone reporting. It provides the means to not only monitor and control all project activities and their outcomes but also provides opportunities for a so-called trend analysis. This allows for root cause analysis to establish what the real reasons are why, for example, something has gone wrong or why errors occurred, and then take appropriate actions to avoid these from happening again.

The overall goals and CSFs for the Atomic Host project are:

Goal 1: Introduce an Innovation Scorecard System for Atomic Host: Container Build Process
   CSF1: Produce high level project documents.
Goal 2: Container Automation Build Process
   CSF1: Develop/buy automation tool and implement it.
   CSF2: Improve way of working.
   CSF3: Improve the Design and Container Build process reporting to improve the communication flow.
   CSF4: Effective Dependency Management during Container Build Process.
Managing the key stakeholders within this project is paramount to its successful

completion. The iScorecard Team conducted a stakeholder analysis and identified the following key stakeholders associated with this project/the Container Rebuild process as follows:

- Container owners
- Container team
- Program manager
- QE
- Release team
- Development team

7.4   Automation Tool

The Container Team in Red Hat has been managing the development of containers (units of software) for a long time. This included some important development work to create a number of new 'container images' for use in a Red Hat initiative known as RHEL 8. New technology was developed that was associated with and related to resolving issues concerned with the maintenance of these images and ensuring long term viability. In addition, consideration was given to infrastructure development to support system developers. Developers often got side-tracked by a plethora of E-mails and other forms of communication received and this distracted them from focusing on the development work. As a direct result of these interventions and based on some earlier automation tool development work, this idea for a fully automated development tool for use in operational environments was progressed further to get this ready for practical deployment. Whilst this work continued, something positive and in their favour happened to this team: they became part of a team in Red Hat known as the Cyborg Team. The Cyborg Team's remit was to find a suitable solution as far as process automation was concerned. The senior manager in charge of the container team decided that this provided the company with a unique opportunity to develop this automation tool for use in RHEL 8. The container team continued with the previous automation tool work they had already completed but also engaged in activities that led to further work being done in this area within their new work environment. As such, it was a win-win situation for all parties involved. At the beginning, they had a requirement for certain simple 'bots' (a basic unit—a container that performs tasks that can be handled by a junior member of staff). Automated processes would have allowed them to compile, build and deploy their code (s) to their production compute platforms (software development pipeline). The Container Team made good use of another tool known as Celery (an 'open' source used in production systems to process up to a million tasks a day). This system focuses on real time operations. Tasks can be executed asynchronously (in the background) or synchronously (wait unit ready). In addition, one of the already deployed 'bots' was set up to ensure that all necessary communications between the other 'bots' and the Container Team (using Celery) could take place as intended and needed, in a timely manner. These so-called 'bots' were created to agglomerate individual things that already existed, for example, tools such as 'build' and 'errata'. So how is the automation tool used in practice?

This newly developed, tried and tested, automation tool was first applied in practice in the RHEL Atomic Host version 7.6.2. The official launch was at the beginning of 2019. The aim of the tool was to minimise and simplify efforts and time needed during the 'build' process. An issue tracker system called JIRA was employed to support the automation process. It allowed issues to be raised so members of the development team, for example, can investigate any issues raised and resolve these in a timely manner. This approach allowed the status of issues to be tracked to ensure that these were completed effectively and efficiently. The adoption of the automation tool achieved higher levels of economies of scale. Previously, many people were involved and engaged, for example, in the resolution of reported issues. Owners of these issues had to investigate raised issues to quite some detailed level, and this often led to repetitive rebuilds. Available resources were not used as best as possible, and this lengthy process led to higher levels of frustration amongst the development teams. A large volume of associated communications necessary to resolve the issues added to the timely delay of resolving issues. The main aim and objective of the automation tool were both achieved though the adoption of a lean, agile, and streamlined automation tool that reduced, for example, the steps needed to resolver reported issues. In addition, the automation tool reduced the high levels of communications that took place in the manual system and replaced this with a 'minimum and vital level of communication' approach. As a result, the issues were resolved in a cost-effective way that achieved maximum productivity and minimum wasted effort.

7.5   Project Schedule

The implementation of the automation tool was planned to be completed in three rounds (Table 7.2). The early build in Round 1 was going to be done manually to ensure that, overall, the RHEL Atomic Process was not interrupted. The final build was completed non-manually (automatically). Then it was planned to build containers automatically in upcoming rounds.

Table 7.2 Time schedule of container rebuild innovation process

	Round 1 RHEL Atomic Host version 7.6.2	Round 2 RHEL Atomic Host version 7.6.3	Round 3 RHEL Atomic Host version 7.6.4
Early build	January 8th 2019	February 19th 2019	April 2nd 2019
Final build	January 22nd 2019	March 4th 2019	April 16th 2019

The effectiveness and efficiency quality of the current process was measured with the help of a research questionnaire and by conducting some face-to-face interviews. It was anticipated to ascertain some basic and some more in-depth data so it was possible for the iScorecard Team to develop and roll-out appropriate performance measures to show evidence of improvements 'before' and 'after' changes to working practices were introduced. A statistical analysis was carried out to enable the production of statistical and graphical performance presentations.

7.6   Assumptions

As is good practice in project management, the iScorecard Team developed a list of assumptions associated with the successful completion of this project. As can be expected from a project of this size, the number of assumptions was limited but fit for intended purpose. The four identified assumptions are described in more detail below:

Assumption 1:   Members of the Red Hat team were sufficiently committed and motivated to complete this project in a timely manner and full support was provided by key stakeholders within Red Hat.

All engaged Red Hat staff participated in this project during their normal working hours, so it was not necessary to measure Full Time Equivalent (FTE) and associated labour costs unless this formed part of a metric, for example, that measured financial performance and/or staff productivity levels. In addition, an external specialist project management consultant was hired (paid for by the Czech Funding Agency) to join the iScorecard Team (two current members made up of a full time University faculty member paid by the University and a part-time M.Sc. student paid from the research grant). The research team made up of Red Hat staff and the iScorecard Team identified key project stakeholders at the start of the project and engaged these in such a way that they provided full support for the research project and dedicated use of the necessary project resources in a timely manner (see Assumption 2 below).

Assumption 2: Shareholders buy-in was secured before launching the innovation project and it is not considered essential to this project to measure the level of support in a separate metric.

Stakeholder management is a critical part of any project irrespective of the project size. When conducted appropriately and aligned to the planned outcomes of the project, it can make a difference to the successful delivery of the project. The iScorecard Team considered that, for a project of this size, it was necessary to engage the key stakeholders but not to perform performance measurements to analyze and evaluate stakeholder performance. In essence, the key and main stake-holder for this project was the CEO of Red Hat in Brno, Czech Republic. He was kept up to date by the iScorecard Team in the form of regular dashboard reports and personal phone calls/face to face discussions. Stakeholder engagement was important for this project. It is of paramount importance to manage the actual engagement with stakeholders and not so much the stakeholders themselves. As such, there was limited scope and need for any prolonged and relevant stakeholder engagement measurement. The focus of the research project was on measuring how successful the delivered innovations of this project have been.

Assumption 3: Communication between members of the whole Innovation Team members was measured through the project's 'Action List' and 'Business as Usual' (BAU) and not within the Innovation Scorecard process.

The iScorecard Team considered that the effectiveness of all communications between the whole team, senior management in Red Hat and key stakeholders was part of the day to day running of the project. It was decided to use the Project Action List (Table 7.3) to establish how good and effective all communications were between the various parties involved in the project. Included in this process were the regular project review meetings, interactive phone conversations between team members and other electronic communications. In addition, key members of the project team regularly reviewed project documentation such as the Project Plan, Project Schedule, Project Definition Document, Issues and Risks register,

Table 7.3 Project Action List

Date	Status	Action no.	Detail	Owner	Deadline
2.1.2019	Open	1	Produce high level project documents—Project Definition Document, Issues and Risks Register, Change Control Process, Project Action List	Student	8.1.2019
9.1.2019	Open	2	To see the senior manager and PGM to talk about the documents	Leader	13.1.2019
14.1.2019	Open	3	Get in touch with expert on statistics, arrange consultation on questionnaire	Professor	18.1.2019
16.1.2019	Open	4	Creation Questionnaire	Student	20.1.2019
23.1.2019	Open	5	Creation Metrics	Leader	27.1.2019
27.1.2019	Open	6	Feedback on Metrics and complete target values	Student	11.2.2019
1.2.2019	Open	7	To arrange The Project Definition Workshop	Leader	16.2.2019
12.2.2019	Open	8	To meet with Red Hat and asked them if they want a monthly Status Report	Student	19.2.2019
20.2.2019	Open	9	Creation of monthly Status Report	Student	28.2.2019
1.3.2019	Open	10	Creation history of the tool and describing of metrics	Student	20.3.2019

Documentation register and Change Control Process. This provided appropriate means for focused communications between people. It strengthened the efficiency and effectiveness of the various types of communications that took place during the life cycle of this project.

7.7   Communication Flow

The iScorecard Team considered that it was necessary to put in place simple but effective communication channels to allow for faster and more focused communications between all project team members and key stakeholders. Quality and speed of communications were considered key criteria to achieve optimum performance. Figure 7.4 shows the adopted communication flow process for this project. All Red Hat teams and the iScorecard Team report to the Red Hat Programme Manager. All team leaders communicate directly with the Programme Manager and team leaders can then communicate with their individual team members. This approach was considered most appropriate for this type of research project. The iScorecard Team works closely with the external team and this enables them to communicate simultaneously with both the Programme Manager and individual technical teams. Direct communications with senior management are also an integral part of the communication process. They usually communicate via e-mails as a daily routine and arrange meetings with the Red Hat Teams when it is needed. All lines of communication follow the hierarchical structure below.

7.8   Data Collection, Analysis, Evaluation and Metrics

Following the establishment of the Atomic Host's project goals, objectives and critical success factors, a metric solution was designed as an information support, for example, for making decisions. It was a necessary requirement to modify the initial Innovation Scorecard system and approach to make it fit for the intended purpose and to ensure that this approach would work in a typical agile software development work environment. Within three rounds (RHEL 7.6.2, 7.6.3 and 7.6.4, see below for details) of the Atomic Host project, between January 2019 and April 2019, the Innovation Scorecard was designed, implemented, and verified as working in practical environments.

The number of metrics or performance measurements needed, for example, for the Atomic Host project, was dependent on the project scope and customer expectations. Kaplan and Norton (1996) suggest that 20 metrics are sufficient for any strategic engagement. This appears to be reasonable but not realistic. Their work was based on management thinking in the late 1990s/early 2000 and can only act as a guideline as the business world has changed, in areas such as IT and Software Development. A predetermined number of metrics should not be set without giving proper thought to what metrics will be needed, why they are needed and what benefit each of the applied metrics will add to the anticipated project outcome. Each work

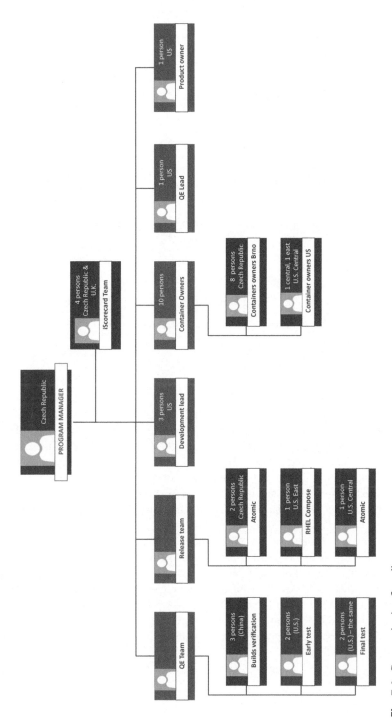

Fig. 7.4 Communication flow diagram

Table 7.4 Innovation metrics

	Metric number/name	Target
Inputs	I01—Working activities structure	Reduce manual repetitive work
	I02—Blocked time	Minimize
Process	P01—Number/weight of errors during implementation	Minimise
Outputs	O01—Number of requests for automation tool changes	Max. 1 radical/10 incremental
	O02—Number of due (priority) activities	Minimise
Results	R01—Job Satisfaction	Increase
	R02—Saved resources	Maximum of Time

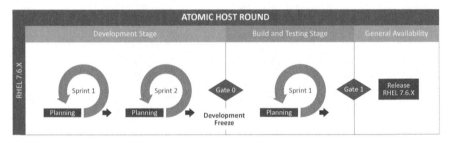

Fig. 7.5 Stage-gate Innovation Scorecard model for Atomic Host

engagement is different so there cannot and should not be a 'one size fits all' approach. In the context of the Atomic Host project, the iScorecard Team considered and developed an appropriate number of metrics (Table 7.4) fit only for the Atomic Host project. This ensured that Red Hat would receive value for money and a good return on their initial investment, for example, in the form of innovative ways of working, reducing unnecessary processes and creating a new confidence in their customer base that Red Hat are delivering industry best practice solutions to customers' desired or required business needs.

The following 'structures' are presentations of each metric description, used in the context of Rounds 1–3 (RHEL 7.62, 7.6.3 and 7.6.4) of the Atomic Host project. This includes the name of the metric and the characteristics of each metric, including, where appropriate, information about when and under what conditions the measurement has been applied. Tables contain measured values from individual versions or values before and after automation. As far as possible there are comments on the results of each version or the results before (Gate 0) and after the introduction of the tool (Gate 1—see Fig. 7.5).

7.8.1 Input Metrics

I01—Working Activities Structure
This particular metric analysed and evaluated the typical working activities structure of seven Container Team Members (CTM) before and after the automation tool implementation. The purpose was to present the impact of automation on the structure where repetitive manual work should be eliminated in favour of other (priority/non-priority) tasks. This qualitative data was obtained through the application of a questionnaire and structured interviews completed before and after the execution of the innovation project. Target values were set by trends (i.e., to reduce manual repetitive work in favour of other priority tasks) as Red Hat currently uses an Agile approach in development and across the company world-wide.

Individual activities in Table 7.5 specifically include the following activities:

Activity 1—Developing new features in the automation system.
Activity 2—Resolving issues in the automation.
Activity 3—Performing manual steps in case of issues.
Activity 4—Communicating with programme management.
Activity 5—Making sure that the builds are done on time.
Activity 6—Building container images using the latest content available.
Activity 7—Making sure the latest build is ready to be shipped (advisory has the build attached and is in state ON_QE).

It was ascertained by the iScorecard Team, based on the outcome of a questionnaire, how much time container team members spent on individual activities. This investigation revealed what their working hours/structure was before and after the implementation of the automation tool. The assumption was a range in % based on 8 h working day/40 h week from Monday to Friday. The idea was to show the impact of automation on the structure where repetitive manual work should be eliminated by the implementation of the tool in practice.

Before the automation all team members had at least one activity in the range, in % terms, such as bigger than 20–0. The purpose of the tool was to minimize these activities and get them to work automatically. For activities 1, 3, 4 and 7, all members of the team 'experienced reductions' within a range of 20–0 after automation of the tool. For the remainder of the activities, numbers 2, 5 and 6 showed associated reductions based on six out of seven people. Collected and analyzed results confirmed that an overall total of five out of seven people, will be able to take on board for example, higher priority tasks in addition to their normal workload, as a direct result of the achieved reduction in repetitive work. This will lead to increases and improvements in productivity levels within their work areas. It will also enable them to focus their attention on new projects or other work activities. In addition,

Table 7.6 Blocked time (hours)	Before	RHEL 7.6.2	RHEL 7.6.3	RHEL 7.6.4
	8–10	8	0.17 (=10 min)	0

with the extra time now being available for other activities, it is also possible to help and support other colleagues with the work these need to deliver. The impact of automation through the implementation of a tool in practice on the work of individual container team members was that it eliminated manual labour, which was one of the main goals of this implementation. It is possible to state that the implementation of an Innovation Scorecard was successful and effective, fulfilled the goal for which it was designed and met expectations.

I02—Blocked Time (Delays)

This metric measured the so-called blocked time when people were waiting for responses from other team members. It was used to measure 'before' and 'after' any changes had been implemented, and after each cycle had been completed. The target value was set to 0 h after three cycles (Table 7.6). The above-mentioned issues were solved by applying the automation tool. A lot of valuable time was saved by adopting this approach. In turn, this allowed team members to focus their attention more on the work they needed to do. This resulted in a significant reduction in the time it took other people to respond to questions asked. Before the innovation was implemented, team members typically were waiting almost 8 h to receive information that they asked for such as information about 'container' issues raised during January 2019. After the automation, this time was reduced to 0 in RHEL 7.6.4. As such, the automation tool saved resources as the number of people needed to resolve any of the typical issues was reduced from ten people to two people, freeing up people's time to, for example, take on board additional work. Levels of frustration were also reduced as raised issues were now addressed and managed much faster and more effectively.

7.8.2　Process Metrics

P01—Number/Weighting of errors during implementation

This metric measured the number and importance of failures within the automation tool implementation (Table 7.7). This metric is applied after each cycle during the implementation by using the following scale to evaluate the importance of instances:

Table 7.9 Number of due (priority) activities

	Before	After
Container Team Member 1	5	0
Container Team Member 2	2	0
Container Team Member 3	4	1
Container Team Member 4	3	1
Container Team Member 5	1	0
Container Team Member 6	1	0
Container Team Member 7	2	0

Table 7.7 Number/weight of errors during implementation

	RHEL 7.6.2		RHEL 7.6.3		RHEL 7.6.4	
	Baseline	Target	Baseline	Target	Baseline	Target
Critical	2	0	0	0	1	0
Medium	7	5	1	5	3	0
Low	4	8	1	8	1	8

- Critical—automatic tool is stopped, and Container Build Process needs to be finalized manually.
- Medium—automatic tool is stopped, and the Container Team can reactivate the process again.
- Low—some bugs can be fixed immediately, and the process can continue.

The initial application of the automation tool generated some errors. There were two critical errors which caused the automation tool to stop functioning. As a result, the automatic container build process was stopped because of these errors, and people reverted to applying the previous manual system until all errors were fixed and the automation tool was brought back into action. The team learned a few lessons and took these on board. As a result, the team were able to avoid any further occurrences of this nature in future. And should this happen again, they were now in a much better position to deal with these unplanned and unforeseen instances.

7.8.3   Output Metrics

O01—Number of requests for Automation Tool Changes
This metric evaluated the implemented automation tool as far as the current state is concerned (Table 7.8). Normal practice is to measure the results after each cycle. Requested changes were made up of two different types, namely radical and incremental tool change requests. Each of the two types of requests were considered and evaluated regarding their suitability and relevance. It was only then that 'approved' changes to the automation tool were implemented and reviewed afterwards in the form of measuring how successful their implementation has been. This included all three areas (RHEL 7.6.2, 7.6.3 and 7.6.4).

Table 7.8 Number of requests for automation tool changes

	RHEL 7.6.2		RHEL 7.6.3		RHEL 7.6.4	
	Baseline	Target	Baseline	Target	Baseline	Target
Radical	2	1	1	1	1	1
Incremental	2	10	0	10	0	10

Table 7.10 Job Satisfaction

	Before	After
Container Team Member 1	8	8
Container Team Member 2	9	8
Container Team Member 3	8	10
Container Team Member 4	7	10
Container Team Member 5	6	7
Container Team Member 6	8	10
Container Team Member 7	9	10

O02—Number of due (priority) Activities

This metric measured the progress made in the working activities structure, with particular emphasis on the impact 'saved time' has on due (priority/non-priority) activities compared to the current state. The metric was applied before any innovation was launched and again after any automation tool implementation. A decreasing trend was set (Table 7.9) as a target value for the Container Team Members (CTM). As a direct result, it was now possible to measure the impact the saved time had on the priority tasks that the team members had to complete in accordance with their job descriptions. Also included were non-priority tasks that would normally not have sufficient time for to complete. Measuring how successful these activities have been confirmed that progress was made to improve the timely completion of priority work activities at both priority and low priority levels. Substantial time savings were achieved through this innovation, and this led to team members being able to fulfil their jobs more effectively and efficiently and to apply saved time in other areas such as team management, leadership and taking on board additional tasks.

7.8.4   Result (Outcome) Metrics

R01—Job Satisfaction

This metric measures the job satisfaction levels (Table 7.10) within the Container Team Members (CTM) in relation to their work activities. Data will be collected through the application of semi-structured interviews with the community of practice and the completion of a research questionnaire. Job satisfaction is measured by using a 10-point Likert scale, applied to measure the 'before' and 'after' outcomes (manual versus automation) of the container rebuild process. A job satisfaction scale ranging from 1 (very dissatisfied) to 10 (very satisfied) was applied. The results from the

Table 7.11 Saved resources

	Before	After
Build process duration	45 * 14 = 630 min (10.5 h)	45 min
Communication	15 * 14 = 210 min (3.5 h)	15 min
Total	840 min = 14 h	60 min = 1 h
Saved resources (time)	13 h	

application of this metric suggest that most team members' job satisfaction levels increased following the introduction of the automation. This further suggests that the change from manual to automatic was received favourably by most teams. The introduction of the tool automation had high expectations, and these have been met generally, indicating that the ways of working shift produced positive operational results. Team members feel that they are now able to make good use of the extra time they have gained through this automation solution to spend, for example, on new features or people management. The automation tool, as it is now, is fit for its intended purpose and as such it is possible to confirm that that the automation roll-out has been successful and that the job satisfaction levels of its users have increased as a direct result.

R02—Saved resources
This metric was concerned with improving the efficiency of the overall container rebuild process, with particular emphasis on improving effective communications and a reduction in the build process duration (Table 7.11). Improvements how to make communications more effective, were measured by the time saved using the automation tool as this included automated reporting. In addition, the build process duration was measured before and after the automation was introduced. This focused on how much time was needed to, for example, to rebuild containers in each process cycle. It was then possible to multiply the number of containers build in each cycle by the time/build process duration to arrive at before and after figures. As can be seen from the outcome of just one process duration, significant time and efforts were saved through automation: the build process was reduced from 10.5 h to just 45 min, the communication process from 3.5 h to just 15 min and the result was a total saving of 13 h.

7.9   Results and Lessons Learned

The Innovation Scorecard was designed, implemented, has been verified that it works in practice and its viability and reliability have been established. Innovation Scorecard was implemented in process innovation, within one Red Hat project known as "Atomic Host". The partially considered objectives for this master thesis were to understand work processes and how Red Hat operates in general. It was necessary to research the theory of what was already known about the subject matter under investigation and to modify the Innovation Scorecard system and approach to make it fit for the intended purpose and use within an Agile Software Development work environment. This included modifications relating to the existing Agile Methodology in operation within Red Hat in addition to further adjustments as far as the innovation approach was concerned. This approach ensured that the concept of an Innovation Scorecard was aligned with the day-to-day operations of Red Hat's Agile Methodology. It was thus possible to implement the proposal for the introduction of an Innovation Scorecard system into the live working environment of Red Hat without disrupting the "business as usual" work activities. Early feedback from the

Table 7.5 Working activities structure (range in %)

	CTM 1		CTM 2		CTM 3		CTM 4		CTM 5		CTM 6		CTM 7	
	Before	After	Before	After	Before	After	Before	After	Before	After	Before	After	Before	After
Activity 1	80–60	20–0	100–80	20–0	40–20	20–0	20–0	20–0	80–60	20–0	60–40	20–0	20–0	20–0
Activity 2	40–20	20–0	40–20	100–80	20–0	20–0	40–20	20–0	60–40	20–0	40–20	20–0	40–20	20–0
Activity 3	20–0	20–0	20–0	20–0	20–0	20–0	20–0	20–0	20–0	20–0	20–0	20–0	40–20	20–0
Activity 4	20–0	20–0	40–20	20–0	20–0	20–0	20–0	20–0	20–0	20–0	20–0	20–0	40–20	20–0
Activity 5	20–0	20–0	20–0	20–0	20–0	20–0	20–0	20–0	80–60	60–40	20–0	20–0	20–0	20–0
Activity 6	20–0	20–0	20–0	20–0	20–0	20–0	20–0	20–0	60–40	40–20	20–0	20–0	20–0	20–0
Activity 7	20–0	20–0	20–0	20–0	20–0	20–0	20–0	20–0	20–0	20–0	20–0	20–0	20–0	20–0

Atomic Host team indicated that the implementation of the Innovation Scorecard system yielded some positive results and that no further modifications were considered necessary to improve it.

One of the Atomic Host teams, known as the Container Team, benefited from the implementation of the Innovation Scorecard. Performance reviews were conducted and the outcomes, based on applying some measurement metrics, suggest that the modus operandi within this team improved significantly. Manual operations were integrated into existing fully automated working practices with the result that duplications of effort were eliminated and or at least improved upon. This resulted in reduced efforts required by the team to carry out certain activities. In turn, this made it possible to team members to be freed up to undertake other or additional tasks, adding further value to the introduction of the Innovation Scorecard within Red Hat. It resulted in significant time savings in terms of efforts employed and it was possible for the team to re-deploy these resources elsewhere in the business. For example, previously mentioned activities 1, 2, 4 and 7 now benefited from a reduction in team members after the tool was automated. This was one of the main goals of the tool application in practice and results suggest that this goal was achieved. For example, a set time delay metric was employed to assess how much time could be saved through the application of the Innovation Scorecard concept. The practical application of this tool met customer expectations leading to a total cancellation of any time delay. A by-product of this experience was the creation of new user perspectives in areas such being creative and innovative. It appeared that Red Hat staff started to talk to each other more. This created new opportunities for working together much more closely and better understand how to build better innovative products for the benefit of Red Hat's customer base.

It can be concluded that the Innovation Scorecard tool has made a major contribution towards reducing the number of errors experienced in some areas of software development such as the Atomic Host. Error reduction target values were achieved over and above any set limit. When new mechanisms were introduced by the Container Team, outside the Innovation Scorecard scope, it became obvious that error values increased. This is a normal and expected behaviour and this provides further evidence in support of an Innovation Scorecard system to combat these issues. It is suggested that an Innovation Scorecard approach adds value to the modus operandi of Container Teams in software development areas.

In the case of requirements, they were those that would in the next version facilitate or improve the further functioning and effectiveness of the tool itself. These were operational changes, but they were successful because the automation of the system went well and the entire process is now being performed automatically, which was the goal of implementing automation info practice.

Due priority activities were gradually reduced as a direct result of saved time. The aim of the tool application in practice was to reduce the manual work of individual members. This goal was achieved, and the time individual members saved can be used on other projects or any related work areas. Another priority metric was Job Satisfaction. It appeared that the Container Team were relatively satisfied with the work they were doing before any changes were introduced. After the introduction of the Innovation Scorecard tool, greater Job Satisfaction levels were identified amongst staff following the outcomes of some research that included team members. Being allowed to be creative and to become innovative leads to higher levels of Job Satisfaction.

The build process was a manual operation that greatly benefited from the Innovation Scorecard process introduction. All work until then was conducted manually. Fully automating this process led to significant reduction in efforts needed by the Container Team opening new opportunities to reassign resources to other areas of the business without affecting the Container Build work area.

The Innovation Scorecard tool has made a significant contribution to improve the efficient and effective operations within Software Development in IT companies such as Red Hat. The outcomes from this research suggest teams such as Container Teams would benefit from a wider roll out of this system. Economies of scale can be achieved in terms of reducing manual efforts and then re-allocating saved resources to support other business areas. It is confirmed that the concept of Innovation Scorecard works both in theory and practice. This will be of great value and benefit to both the community of practice and academia. It is hoped that this research has brought theory and practice much closer together.

Summary of Benefits:

- Improved communications leading to improved development and build of innovative products and services.
- Container build process reduced by 13 h, opening-up new opportunities to reassign resources to other areas of the business.
- Significant reduction in duplication of errors and reworks.
- Innovation Scorecard aligned with existing Agile Methodology without disrupting 'business as usual'.

Reference

Kaplan, R. S., & Norton, D. P. (1996). *The Balanced Scorecard: Translating strategy into action.* Harvard Business School Press.

Case Study 2: Continuous Integration

8

8.1   Introduction and Executive Summary

Red Hat is a leading provider of so-called open source and Linux operating systems which are based on making original source codes freely available. Red Hat's mission is "to be the catalyst for customers, contributors and partners in order to create improved technology based on an open-source principle". To achieve this mission, Red Hat are applying a so-called "agile" approach for their software development projects to get the right work done faster.

The Continuous Integration (CI) case study's focus was on the introduction of an Innovation Scorecard concept within a life working environment within Red Hat Czech in Brno, Czech Republic. It included measuring how successful, for example, implemented process innovations or changes at Red Hat had been, based on "before" and "after" case study output data. This project was one of three projects that make up the overall Innovation Scorecard research project (the first and initial pilot case study was known as Atomic Host. Its primary focus was on some automation process. The third and final case study was known as Global Wi-Fi rollout and involved further work process and people management process improvements).

The Innovation Scorecard process was made up of the following structure: Goals—Critical Success Factors—KPIs—Selecting Metrics—Target Values. The starting point was the setting of the goals to be achieved through the Innovation Scorecard application in practice. The next step was to identify the critical success factors that were necessary for the project to achieve its mission. Key performance indicators are also associated with critical success factors, representing a measurable value that would demonstrate the success of meeting the objectives set throughout the project. A very significant part of this work was the determination of metrics and their target values. Metrics were used to express innovative goals that had to be clear and flawless and at the same time achievable. It was not important how many metrics were set but their quality and overall contribution to the successful implementation of the Innovation Scorecard design was most important. It was precisely the determination of the right metrics and their targets that were important to achieve the set goals.

The Innovation Scorecard model was implemented in structured and logical order. This was the only way to guarantee success. For this reason, the methodology or approach of the selected Innovation Scorecard was divided into five phases controlled by four gates to ensure a smooth implementation. To adapt the Innovation Scorecard system to specific Continuous Integration processes, only the following four stages were evaluated and considered to be the most appropriate:

• Stage 1: Idea Generation
• Stage 2: Idea Development
• Stage 3: Implementation
• Stage 4: Post-implementation Review

Due to the nature of the work, the iScorecard team engaged in problem-solution activities to ensure that the project was delivered within agreed timescales. To plan, organize, monitor, and control the whole project, the iScorecard team conducted the following activities to manage this project:

• Regular monthly progress review meetings
• Production of 'minutes of meetings'
• Ad hoc face to face meetings with Red Hat
• Regular telephone calls with the project manager and one of Red Hat's internal software development teams known as 'Leapp'
• Preparation and Circulation of monthly 'dashboard reports'
• Documentation reviews

The biggest gains were delivered in 'changes to customer requirements' during the development cycle. Red Hat decided to adopt a so-called "Scrum" agile project management approach as this was most suitable for their current modus operandi (Scrum is made up of some working practices used in agile project management that are based on daily communications and a flexible approach to assess plans). Each of this research project's phases was managed applying so-called "short sprints" that are typical for use in software development to get things done quickly and efficiently without hindrance and interruptions by external interventions. A complete analysis of the current Red Hat processes and procedures revealed potential areas for process improvements across many disciplines. This work was vital for the development of the Innovation Scorecard's team approach and the design, development and roll out of the most appropriate stage/gate approach (dividing the project into more manageable phases, see above).

In collaboration with one of Red Hat's internal software development teams (Leapp team), an investigation was conducted to assess what errors needed to be fixed within the CI process. This set the foundation for assessing what process improvements were deemed necessary to fix these issues and how the results could be measured in terms of their successful implementation. It was interesting to note that Red Hat's way of working highlighted many areas that could be improved by the iScorecard team such as communications between various team members, time taken to resolve reported errors/bugs and empowering people to make decisions. Early results indicated that the introduction of the Innovation Scorecard made some significant process improvements to Red Hat's 'ways of working'.

In summary, the outcome of this research made a major contribution to improve the modus operandi within Red Hat. For example, the time it took Red Hat staff in the past to generate new ideas was reduced significantly. Communication between team members were improved by allowing staff to communicate more directly without the need to refer to senior management first. And finally, some of the software development processes were changed and strengthened with the result that the time it took to complete certain tasks was substantially reduced.

8.2 Background Information

8.2.1 Key Terms and Definitions

CI/CD is a method to frequently deliver apps to customers by introducing automation into the stages of app development. The main concepts attributed to CI/CD are continuous integration, continuous delivery, and continuous deployment (Fig. 8.1).

Continuous Integration (CI) is a phase in the software development cycle where code from different team members or different features are integrated together. This usually involves merging code (integration), building the application and carrying out basic tests all within an ephemeral environment.

Continuous Delivery usually means a developer's changes to an application are automatically bug tested and uploaded to a repository (like GitHub or a container registry), where they can then be deployed to a live production environment by the operations team. It's an answer to the problem of poor visibility and communication between development and business teams. To that end, the purpose of continuous delivery is to ensure that it takes minimal effort to deploy new code.

Continuous Deployment (the other possible "CD") can refer to automatically releasing a developer's changes from the repository to production, where it is usable by customers. It addresses the problem of overloading operations teams with manual

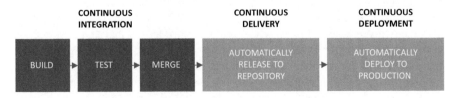

Fig. 8.1 CI/CD pipeline (https://www.redhat.com/en/topics/devops/what-is-ci-cd)

processes that slow down app delivery. It builds on the benefits of continuous delivery by automating the next stage in the pipeline.

8.2.2   Red Hat's New CI/CD Vision

To deliver code changes faster, with fewer errors and at lower costs
The long-term target presented by Red Hat for the Continuous Integration and Continuous Delivery (CI/CD) project was based on providing the customer with a response to a new code as quickly as possible. To achieve this objective, the CI process had to incorporate reliable testing of any 'embedded new code'. The applied CI approach provided rapid feedback to allow for any defect correction to the 'code base'. This included more in-depth testing to generate higher levels of reliability and validity. The theory was that once a high-quality new code had been produced that did not generate any negative feedback, the associated Continuous Delivery (CD) process could be engaged to deliver the new code to the customer.

Due to work pressures, Red Hat staff were not always able to share the necessary project data with the iScorecard team when needed. This led to some serious delays that ultimately led to the abolition of the planned CD initiative.

8.3   Current CI Process

To understand why Red Hat wanted to introduce changes, it is necessary to describe how the CI process works and what problems occurred by default. As part of the Continuous Integration process, Red Hat uses a distributed versioning system known as GitHub to record changes in files. GitHub is version control system that allows to work together with other developers. With GitHub it can be seen what others are working on, review their code without traveling a thousand miles. Unlike centralized systems, the user is not downloading only the latest version of the file but represents the entire repository. In a 'collapse' (this term is used in software development and means, in this context, to compress or shorten a hierarchy so that only the roots of each branch are visible), the data can then be restored from the user. Red Hat's approach is to share project details, for example, with developers, and it is for this reason that they apply the so-called GitHub approach. GitHub is an automated system that can remember occurred changes. The issue with GitHub is that it is an automated system and there appears to be some room for further improvement to enhance this system. If a new code is generated GitHub takes a "picture" of all the files at any given time and saves references that relate to this snapshot (Fig. 8.2). If there is no change in the code, it does not create a new record, but merely refers to the previous identical record that has already been saved. The next step in the CI process is to perform testing. Testing is a process for obtaining information about the characteristics and status of a system to determine if the system is operating as specified in the proposal.

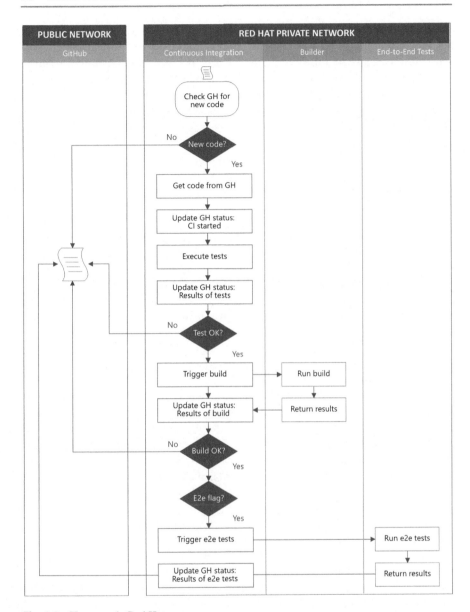

Fig. 8.2 CI process in Red Hat

A typical test performed on integration servers is the unit test. If there was a change in any of the codes used, the test starts automatically. This test provides detailed feedback on how the code works. If the code passes the unit test, the "Triggers Build" runs, which allows to set how often the task will run. Then all that remains to be done are the test runs.

The last step before 'final saving', is adding a "post-Build" step. This typically involves specifying where the output results should be sent (usually an E-mail address). Once this step has been completed, it is possible to determine whether the code is active or not. If it is negative, GitHub is updated appropriately. In case it is active, it goes to the last stage of testing using "end to end" (E2E) tests. Running E2E testing enables the final identification of any associated code issues before going 'live'.

8.4   Issues in Current CI Process

Errors happen during the Continuous Integration process. This is often time consuming. The Leapp team, in our CI case study example, captured any known software development issues. This resulted in the development of new ideas how to resolve these problems as fast and as optimally as possible.

One identified problem related to a lack of disk space. Almost all disk space is consumed by previous builds so there was insufficient space for new builds. When an open-source CI integrated server known as 'Jenkins' detects that a disk has run out of capacity, then any copying and E2E tests that merge the system with the 'public' are blocked. This block can be fixed by freeing up available disk space. It becomes a serious issue with an increasing number of new external contributors.

There was room for improvement in this area. Using Jenkins can accelerate the software development process as this system can automate 'build and test' very fast. Another problem, representing medium severity, is the "post-Build" step, as was described in Red Hat's current CI process. If team members wanted to know the details of E2E tests, they had to check the Jenkins system manually. The following medium severity issue was related to the GitHub status. When a job failed before any test was executed, GitHub status was not updated and got stuck on "pending".

This problem occurred when an error was 'embedded' within the code. By looking at the public network, it was not evident that a problem had occurred. Whenever this happened, it was necessary to check the Jenkins system for relevant details, especially who needed to be contacted to obtain further details.

One of the biggest problems was the time spent by engineers to continually fix any errors in the system. Only one engineer was deployed for this work, with no back-up staff in place to step in, for example, during periods of absence. In addition, test results needed to be made available to anyone who opened a so-called 'pull request', important when external contributors were involved. This was not yet possible to implement because the unit tests ran on an internal infrastructure, so it was impossible to publish these tests for security reasons. This issue needed to be fixed as it was time consuming, and this in turn would lead to potential cost savings. The iScorecard team joined the project at this moment in time. The conceptual performance of this team had the future potential to improve efficiency and ultimate competitiveness within the IT and Software Industry in companies other than Red Hat.

8.5   Objectives and Innovation Scorecard Design

The issues with CI described in the previous section led to a change request for an upgrade to the innovation process. It was hoped and anticipated that the process change could solve or at least eliminate some of the issues addressed. These problems needed a lot of maintenance time. This was the reason why Red Hat (CI/CD team is called Leapp team hereinafter) decided to work with the iScorecard team so that this team could help to resolve this issue.

In cooperation with the Leapp team an initial Project Definition Document (PDD) was produced based on a principle known as 'BOSCARD' (see Methodology, Sects. 4.2 and 4.4). A completed PDD can be found in the Appendix section of the methodology, together with other relevant documentation.

The considered objectives for the CI project were:

- Make the process easy to update and fit for its intended purpose
- Reduce or minimise maintenance
- Improve the speed of managing issues
- Reduce engineering input time

Our initial thoughts where metrics should be applied, focused on the following work areas, and produced some high-level measurements:

- To improve 'greatest delivery impact' workflow processes
- To improve the 'software coding' quality inputs and outputs
- To shorten the time to market
- To improve how team members co-ordinated and collaborated their work efforts
- To increase the visibility of the progress status of new features
- To enhance the ability to deploy/release updates at different intervals, with a closer alignment to departmental schedules

The transition from the existing traditional agile to agile CI needed a paradigm shift and it needed a full commitment, for example, from stakeholders, project managers, and developers. Our biggest challenges included the planning of all this and to educate the development teams, explaining the reasons why these changes were considered necessary and the intentions behind the changes. We focused our attention on the two most important aspects: output (or outcomes) and the way the Leapp team created and managed coding at present.

Typical documents created during the project (some documents) are presented in the Appendix section of the methodology:

- Weekly call(s)
- Project Action List (Appendix U)
- The Risk and Issues Register (Appendices V and W)
- Project Schedule (Appendix X)
- Project Definition Document (Appendix AA)

- Change Control Process
- Minutes of Meetings
- Monthly Project Progress Report (Appendix Y)
- Innovation Scorecard Guide
- Innovation Scorecard Data Sheet (Appendix Z)

Within this more complex and long-term project the Innovation Scorecard management control framework was implemented in a well-structured and logical order to guarantee success. To adapt the Innovation Scorecard system to this case study's specific Continuous Integration process, the following four stages only were evaluated and considered to be the most appropriate (Fig. 8.3):

- Stage 1: Idea Generation
- Stage 2: Idea Development
- Stage 3: Implementation
- Stage 4: Post-Implementation Review (PIR)

A weighted system of metrics for use in each gate was proposed by Red Hat's Leapp team project manager. The project manager had a number of questions to ask such as: *"To make a Go decision, does it mean that all metrics have to achieve the target value of 100% level, or is, let's say, 80% enough? If 80%, what metrics can reach this lower level? We should be able to distinguish between 'critical' metrics where 100% achievement of the target values is required and 'not so critical' metrics with lower percentage rates of achievement."* Therefore, especially for Gate 2 and 3, this approach was adopted and implemented.

Another essential point in our discussion with the project manager, was the 'thin border line' between the development and the implementation stage. This was typical for an agile working environment. A typical 'agile mantra' purports *'Done is better than perfect'*. To avoid a so-called cascading or waterfall system, when the implementation stage can start only when the development stage is fully completed, for example, we used a weighted system of metrics in Gate 2. The proof-of-concept that met critical criteria passed the implementation stage. But the valuable feedback and change requests relating to this 'proof-of-concept' were collected. As a direct consequence, both the implementation and enhancement 'proof-of-concept' principles could run in parallel.

The iScorecard Team also presented several suitable and fit for intended purpose measurement metrics to Red Hat staff at a project review meeting. The suggested metrics were discussed and agreed during a project review meeting with the Red Hat team. Several metrics were adopted as suitable to form the core of the Gate 1–3 performance and outcome measurements. Following on from some further and final discussions with the Red Hat team, the final set of metrics, most suitable for use in the Continuous Integration process, were selected and adopted by both the Red Hat and the iScorecard teams.

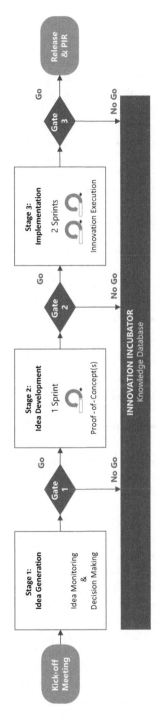

Fig. 8.3 The Innovation Scorecard for the CI project

8.6   Communication Flow

There was a Continuous Communication flow in this project between Red Hat and the Innovation Scorecard team (Fig. 8.4). Regular interactions took place in the form of face to face, telephone, and electronic communications. The Red Hat project manager (PM) oversaw a team of nine people, known as the Leapp team. Red Hat advised that their current team structure could change in line with changing operational requirements. The iScorecard team, made up of members of Brno University of Technology and an external project management specialist consultant, worked with the Red Hat project managers in close co-operation. All lines of communication followed this hierarchical structure. The flow of communication (right information at the right time in the right format to the right people) formed an important part of this project.

The following communication methods were applied in the project:

- Meetings (regular and irregular) with Red Hat and the iScorecard Team
- E-mails
- Monthly Project Progress Reports (Appendix Y)
- Formal and Informal Verbal, Written and Visual Communications
- Workshops, Presentations and Publications
- iScorecard Website

8.7   Data Collection, Analysis, Evaluation and Metrics

8.7.1   Stage 1: Idea Generation

Idea generation represented a collection of ideas designed to improve the CI process. These ideas were analyzed in detail to check and confirm if they met all the right criteria to be considered for adoption.

The CI innovation project was launched following a brainstorming session to generate ideas how to improve the quality of the CI process (measured by the number of errors). These ideas were analyzed in detail to check and confirm if they met all the criteria and could be considered for adoption. The Leapp team created a document called 'Leapp Continuous Integration Status'. The main purpose of this document was to summarize the advantages and disadvantages of all considered ideas. The next step included an analysis of the chosen ideas and to check if these ideas met Red Hat's requirements of "what made an acceptable new idea to achieve innovation". Further checks then confirmed if any considered ideas could be realistically implemented. Any ideas considered not fit for their intended purpose and not meeting Red Hat's requirements were discarded. Any idea that did not pass Stage 1 of the adopted Stage Gate process was not moved forward to Stage 2. Table 8.1 is a summary of the adopted metrics and the associated target values.

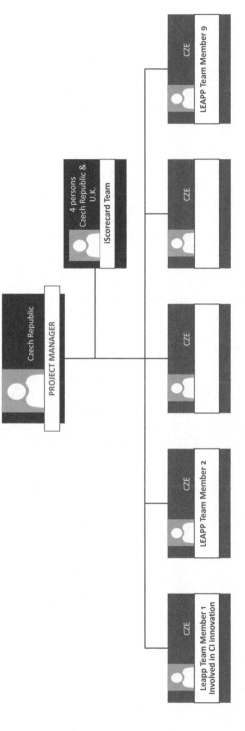

Fig. 8.4 Communication flow diagram

Table 8.1 Metrics for Gate 1

	Metric number/name	Target
Inputs	G1I01—Work Effort for Given Tasks	iScorecard max. 0.8 FTE Red Hat max. 0.25 FTE
	G1I02—Quality of Current CI Process	Minimise blocks
Process	G1P01—Time of Systematic Idea Generation and Evaluation	Max. 1 week
Outputs	G1O01—Quality of Generated Idea(S)	Min. 75%
Results	G1r01—Milestone/Deadline	6th July 2019
	G1R02—Total Cost of Idea Generation Phase	Maximum 50,000 CZK

G1I01—Work Effort for Given Tasks

This metric was designed to help determine how effectively and efficiently human resources had been deployed and how productive and successful the application of the iScorecard team's innovation stage gate process was. The main purpose for deploying and tracking this metric was to focus on the responsibilities of project team members and to establish how they were able to execute their clearly defined responsibilities, using typical project management performance criteria such as time, cost, and quality. In addition, the following Full Time Equivalent (FTE) metric (Table 8.2) was agreed at a follow-on meeting with the Red Hat team.

The earlier referred to and adopted "Leapp CI Status" document was created during the Idea Generation phase of this project. It took two team meetings to develop and finalise this document. The first meeting lasted approximately 10 min and was mainly concerned with some initial "in principle" agreements what information the document should contain and how this document should be used. The second meeting appeared to be much more productive. It lasted for just an hour and the teams involved focused their attention more on, for example, creating error lists (also known as bug lists). This list contained relevant details of all occurring errors within the CI project. In the past, it took one engineer nearly 4 h to produce the same information. It was evident from the outcome of this one exercise that the introduction of innovative ways of working already showed early positive results that suggested what the potential resource savings in Red Hat could be at the end of this project, based on the results of measuring how successful this one innovation has

Table 8.2 Work Effort for Given Tasks

Baseline (FTE)	Inception	Termination
Leapp PM	0.03	0.05
Leapp Team	0.13	0.20
Red Hat Team	0.00	0.00
Red Hat summary	*0.16*	*0.25*
Team Leader	0.30	0.40
Professor	0.30	0.20
Student	0.20	0.40
iScorecard Team summary	*0.80*	*1.00*

been. Overall, this iterative approach helped to produce a valuable document that summarized the identified CI project issues and how to mitigate/resolve the issues. This was of great help to both the project manager and Red Hat's Leapp Team.

Prior the Project Launch, the iScorecard team was already working on creating a necessary document for the CI project—a Project Definition Document (PDD). This document described high details of how this project would be managed, what assumptions were made and what the expected outcomes of the project were. The PDD also described in sufficient detail the suggested metrics for each of the process Gates.

G1I02—Quality of Current CI Process
This is one of the core metrics that were been identified for application within the CI project. Its efficiency was evaluated in two stages: before and after the CI innovation implementation and then at quarter-yearly intervals. Measures that were applied included maintenance time, number of blockages and average time spent on managing blockers. Table 8.3 is a good example of how much time both the Leapp and Red Hat teams spent over a given period to fix errors/bugs including any duplication of effort due to the way the teams were working at the time. Some errors/bugs were of such a nature that it was not possible for the teams to follow the CI process as the errors/bugs needed to be fixed before they could do so. It was frustrating and very time consuming. Some so-called 'features', associated with software development work, also slowed down the teams as far as the CI process was concerned. As can be seen from Table 8.3, bugs occur more often than features. In this example, eight bugs were recorded during this reporting period, and it took the Leapp Team 180 h to repair these, plus the Red Hat team spent an additional 20 h to do the same. In contrast, there were only two features the Leapp Team needed to fix, and this took them 32 h in total. Both areas provide ample opportunities to reduce the time it takes to fix bugs/manage features. This is where the Innovation Scorecard and associated metrics made a substantial difference in terms of reducing error/bug fixing times and proving how successful these changes had been compared to their current way of working in both the Leapp and Red Hat teams.

G1P01—Time of Systematic Idea Generation and Evaluation
This metric was developed to assess and measure how much time it took to generate new ideas that could successfully solve identified issues and problems within the CI process. It was an absolute necessity that any new ideas had to be of high quality and fit for intended purpose and use throughout the CI process. Initially, the Red Hat project manager started the process of coming up with innovative ideas how to

Table 8.3 Lists of errors from January to May

Name	Frequencies	Leapp Team (h)	Red Hat team (h)	Blockage (h)
Bugs	8	180	20	200
Features	2	32	0	32
In total				232

Table 8.4 Time of systematic idea generation and evaluation

Baseline (h)	Leapp PM	Leapp Team	External Red Hat Team
Idea 1 Generation	0.17	2.00	0
Idea 1 Evaluation	0.33	0.17	0
Idea 2 Generation	0.17	2.00	0
Idea 2 Evaluation	1.00	1.00	0
Idea1 in total	0.50	2.17	0
Idea2 in total	1.17	3.00	0

improve current processes. He wanted to make sure that the Leapp team's primary focus was on creating new codes rather than get side-tracked by any distractions that could delay their main work. As a result of this approach, it was possible to create new ideas far more constructively, making the best use of available resources. Two ideas (Table 8.4) from the list of created options were selected. They were considered most suitable to fix most of the identified problems. The first idea was to migrate the maximum number of CI processes to a hosted continuous integration service called Travis CI. This service was used to build and test software projects that were hosted with the help of something known as GitHub (development platform used by software developers to review and build codes). It appeared to the team that this approach could potentially resolve the following associated issues:

- Test results would be visible to everyone involved in the process
- Reduced need for any repairs compared to the current CI process
- Tests run automatically and can run at individual or large group levels
- Reduced likelihood of malicious codes being introduced into the process

The second idea was concerned with improving the original thinking of staying with an open-source automation server (known as Jenkins). This approach, sometimes referred to as the non-human part of the software development process, enabled software developers to reliably build, test and deploy their software. This solution had the advantage of allowing for an endless customization of the associated server. The disadvantages of adopting this approach are twofold. Red Hat associates only would have sight of the test results and it carries a need for substantial regular maintenance related to its infrastructure. The measurement of the idea generating process established that the project manager spent 30 min on developing Idea 1- and 70-min developing Idea 2. In contrast, the Leapp team spent 130 min to assess whether Idea 1 was feasible for application within the CI process. They spent 180 min on assessing whether Idea 2 was feasible. This provided the iScorecard Team with significant statistical evidence on which to base suggestions how this process could be improved, working collaboratively with all parties involved in the CI process.

G1O01—Quality of Generated Idea(s)

This metric was intended to illustrate the expectation, expressed in percentage terms, of how many problems in the CI process could be solved in relation to the number of generated problems. The adoption of this metric carried another benefit. It was possible to measure resource commitment levels in terms of time and inputs needed to resolve problems. This metric's primary focus was on measuring all functionalities irrespective of their difficulty level such as easy or difficult. This ensured that easy functionalities were not completed first at the expense of difficult functionalities. It was also possible that measurement results would be distorted. This would "send the wrong message to senior management". The iScorecard team was asked to apply some form of "weighting" to each functionality to manage this challenge as objectively and effectively as possible. Contrasting views between the main parties concerned developed during the early process stage. The project manager expected that Idea 1 should solve 71% of the identified problems. The Leapp team's view was different. They considered that only 64% of the identified problems associated with Idea 1 would be resolved successfully. As far as Idea 2 was concerned, the project manager did not expect any problem resolution. His reasons for holding this view were manifold:

- Open visibility of unit testing-everyone could see everything at any time resulting in too many interferences
- The automation of build creation may not suit this process
- A reduction of available engineering time due to spending too much time on fixing errors/bugs

The project manager held the view that the Jenkins server could not provide any improvements. The Leapp Team did not share this view. They considered that adopting a Jenkins approach would yield at least 50% improvements to solve problems. This team also rated the second Idea much higher that the project manager. It was based on having access to far more data than the project manager has. This provided the Leapp Team with supportive evidence on which to base their views. This team was more focused on finding innovative solutions that would ultimately improve their modus operandi (Table 8.5).

Table 8.5 Expected quality of the generated ideas

Baseline		Idea 1: Migration from Jenkins to Travis CI		Idea 2: Jenkins's tune-up	
Problem	Weight	Leapp PM	Leapp Team	Leapp PM	Leapp Team
Unit tests	0.5	100%	100%	0%	50%
Build creation	0.1	75%	50%	0%	50%
E2E tests	0.1	0%	0%	0%	50%
Complexity	0.3	45%	30%	0%	50%
Summary		71%	64%	0%	50%

Table 8.6 Total cost of idea generation phase

Baseline	FTE	Average weekly costs (CZK)	Costs (CZK)
iScorecard	0.60	16,500	13,200
Red Hat	0.16	19,500	3087
Summary			16,287

G1R01—Milestone/Deadline

Pace and effectiveness were two of the many components that determine whether a project was going well. It was suggested that there was a need for a metric that measured whether the development phase of an idea was being implemented in time and how successful that implementation had been. The outcome of the applied metric met expected results.

G1R02—Total Cost

This metric measured the money spent during the first phase of the project. This cost tracking was used as a benchmark for future projects and associated phases. The total cost of the idea creation phase was calculated based on the time to complete this project stage. It was measured by multiplying, for example, the hours a person spent on work related to this project. An average hourly associate/senior manager hourly rate was applied to calculate the actual cost to the business for conducting this work. It was then possible to compare the total cost for work done with the set financial limit Red Hat has agreed for this project such as 50,000 CZK. As can be seen from Table 8.6, the total cost incurred did not exceed the budget limit. The iScorecard team ensured, through regular reviews and calculations, that this limit was not exceeded and that it was managed accordingly. This adopted approach ensured that the true cost of innovation in Red Hat was measured for the benefit of senior management so informed business decisions, for example, can be made.

> Note: We applied average weekly labour costs (includes salary and social/health insurance) for confidentiality reasons. In your project you should apply the actual business staff costs to calculate 'actual' costs.

8.7.2   Stage 2: Idea Development

The concept of Idea Development played an important role within the Continuous Integration project. One of its major functions was to explore and establish how the generated ideas from the previous project stage could be suitably integrated into the whole CI process. Another of its functions was to verify and confirm that adopted ideas were fit for their intended purpose and that accepted and implemented ideas improved Red Hat's operational performance. It was possible to measure how successful and effective adopted ideas had been through the application of appropriate measurement techniques such as metrics and statistical analysis. It was thus possible to provide evidence of performance improvement or deterioration on a work

Table 8.7 Metrics for Stage 2

	Metric number/name	Target
Inputs	G2IO1—Work Effort for Given Tasks	iScorecard max. 2 FTE Red Hat max. 1.6 FTE
	G2I02—Number of Proposals from Stage 1	Min. 1
Process	G2P01—Interventions Within the Development Stage by the Innovation Team	Intended max. 1 Unintended max. 5
Outputs	G2O01—Quality of Proof of Concept Offered	Min. 75%
Results	G2R01—Milestone/Deadline	30th July 2019
	G2R02—Total Cost of Idea Development Stage	Maximum 100,000 CZK

area by work area basis. Like the approach considered in Stage 1, the effectiveness and efficiency of investigated current processes was measured objectively through the application of face-to-face interviews with Red Hat staff who were engaged in the associated work activities. The iScorecard team expected that data of different depth levels would be generated by this research. This enabled the team to develop and roll-out appropriate performance measures to show evidence of improvements such as 'before' and 'after' changes to working practices were introduced. Continuity was an important factor within the CI process. This meant that any considered and ultimately selected ideas could proceed to Stage 3 when all selection criteria had been met. To succeed with this approach, the iScorecard team agreed with Red Hat senior management that the development of ideas would be managed through 'sprints' that typically lasted for 2 weeks. So-called integration testing was carried out after every two sprint events. This type of testing was part of a testing sequence that included unit, integration and user acceptance testing to ensure that integrated components worked together as expected and intended. Table 8.7 shows a summary of developed and adopted performance metrics and the target values the iScorecard team set for each of these. Further metrics were considered necessary to measure how successful each innovation had been, a kind of measuring the measurement.

G2IO1—Work Effort for Given Tasks

This metric was very similar to the metric used for Stage 1. Because this was a different process than in the previous Stage, it was appropriate to measure and determine how effectively and efficiently human resources had been deployed. The essence of tracking this metric was to focus on project team members and see how much effort they made to meet the goals set during Gate 2. This metric would measure, with the time individual team members spent on project related activities, expressed in Full Time Equivalent (FTE) terms. The target value of this metric was to reach 1.60 FTE for Red Hat and 2.00 FTE for iScorecard. Table 8.8 includes 'common extension details'. This was agreed at a meeting with Red Hat staff. The reason for this inclusion was that the time spent on this 'common extension' was greater than the work associated with both ideas separately. It describes the ability to

Table 8.8 Work Effort for Given Tasks

Baseline [FTE]	Sprint 1		In total	Target
	Week 1 10.6.2019–14.6.2019	Week 2 17.6.2019–21.6.2019		
iScorecard	1.00	0.85	1.85	2.00
Team Lead	0.40	0.30	0.70	0.80
Professor	0.30	0.25	0.55	0.40
Student	0.30	0.30	0.60	0.80
Red Hat	1.14	0.05	1.19	1.50
Leapp PM	0.01	0.00	0.01	0.20
Leapp Team	1.13	0.05	1.18	1.00
RH Team	0.00	0.00	0.00	0.30

interchange hardware or software in some software development environment without any other code or configuration changes being required. This resulted in zero negative impacts. This extension, used for Travis and Jenkins applications, was 'tried and tested' to confirm if the adoption of these applications generated more stability. Members of the project (Leapp team) spent in total 18 h working on the idea 1 and 5 h for idea 2. Most of the work was done in the first week of the sprint, the second week included only one so-called 'pull request', which was important for assessing whether the ideas involved were compatible for the process.

G2I02—Number of Proposals from Stage 1
This metric measured the number of ideas generated in Stage 1 that had been considered and moved forward to Stage 2 (Idea Development). It was only applied once during Stage 1. The execution was typically conducted prior to the start of Stage 2. The considered ultimate target was to have at least one idea approved and selected. Any selected idea had to be justified. The following two ideas passed the selection process and were considered fit for use throughout the CI process to:

1. Migrate the maximum number of CI processes to a hosted CI service called Travis CI
2. Improve the original thinking of staying with an open-source automation server known as Jenkins

Each of these ideas incorporated expected benefits that were congruent with the idea generating process criteria. As a result, once the idea generating process was completed, a decision was made by the iScorecard team to proceed to Stage 2 as all requirements to move to the next stage were fulfilled.

G2P01—Interventions within the Development Stage by the Innovation Team
This metric was intended to record any intentional or unintentional intervention that arose either from a key stakeholder group in the Red Hat team or from the iScorecard team. It was also important to mention that any intervention had a positive effect on

the CI process and did not harm it in any way. The maximum target values for these metrics were set at five intentional and one unintended intervention. No thoughtful or unintended interventions were recorded during the idea development phase that would significantly change the CI process. As a result, it was reasonable to assume that, in principle, the desired target had been achieved.

G2O01—Quality of Proof of Concept

This metric's primary focus was on the completion of activities that lead to the confirmation and demonstration that this pilot study project's design concept in Innovation Scorecard worked when implemented. This proof of concept (PoC) showed that the Innovation Scorecard team's approach to deliver the 'Continuous Integration Project', from a technological point of view, was feasible. This metric's starting point was based on two ideas that were developed in the previous Stage 2 (Idea Development). These ideas were considered fit for intended purpose, and it was now necessary to confirm that this consideration proved to be true. Proof of concept typically involved the application of two sequential actions. The initial action was concerned with establishing the potential research feasibility. One such review covered the area of application mapping. This was a process used in areas such as IT and software development. It dealt with and established, for example, what the components and interdependencies were within a certain software development area and then 'mapped' these. It provided a kind of 'helicopter' view of any total process. This would aid informed decision making. Provided this first step was completed successfully and produced a positive evaluation in terms of feasibility, the research project was allowed to continue to the second action. This involved moving any considered and confirmed suitable ideas to the implementation phase (Stage 3).

To ensure that the proof of concept continued to stay true to its nature, it was necessary to review the status of the concept after agreed changes were integrated. Essential integration testing was conducted to achieve this. This ensured continuity of quality control and assurance. It was generally considered more effective to conduct measurements after changes were implemented. This was based on the knowledge and experience that not all sprints generated changes. This metric was based on the use of a so-called flexible job board solution that provided the Red Hat team with full visibility of all planned activities. This approach provided opportunities to maximise work output with minimum effort. This metric (Table 8.9) was intended to show how many problems were solved during the

Table 8.9 Offered proof of concept Quality

Baseline		Idea 1: Migration from Jenkins to Travis CI		Idea 2: Jenkins's tune-up	
Problem	Weighting	Leapp PM	Leapp Team	Leapp PM	Leapp Team
Unit tests	0.5	100%	100%	0%	100%
Build creation	0.1	0%	0%	0%	75%
End2End tests	0.1	0%	0%	0%	75%
Complexity	0.3	30%	30%	0%	75%
Summary		59%	59%	0%	88%

proof-of-concept phase. It provided supportive evidence by considering how many ideas were generated in relation to the number of identified associated issues.

An important benefit of this metric was its ability to focus on all features regardless of the difficulty level (easy or difficult). This provided assurance that easy functions were not completed in preference to more difficult functions. Red Hat applied some 'weighting' to certain functions in accordance with their levels of priority. This enabled the iScorecard team to manage this challenge as unbiased and as objectively as possible. Based on the outcome of the feasibility study for considered improvement ideas, the project manager decided that Idea 1 could solve 59% of the identified problems. Red Hat's Leapp team shared the Project Manager's view leading to an agreed implementation of the adopted Idea 1. There was a difference of opinion as far as Idea 2 was concerned. The Project Manger maintained a strong view that the implementation of Idea 2 would not lead to a resolution of identified problems associated with Idea 2. The Leapp team considered that the 'Jenkins' enhancement could potentially solve 88% of the identified issues. This issue was resolved. The Project Manager decided to proceed with his view and that therefore the implementation of Idea 2 did not go ahead. The issue was closed successfully.

The iScorecard team experienced a similar problem during Stage 1 (Idea Generation) as far as the evaluation of the quality of the generated ideas was concerned. It was therefore possible to compare the two metrics and extrapolate relevant information that helped to determine which idea, for example, met the feasibility criteria better in relation to the proof of concept.

In contrast, Migration from Jenkins to Travis CI (Table 8.10) had a 12% lower success rate than the project manager expected. The Leapp team agreed with the Project Manager. In addition, there was a negative deviation between the expected quality of the idea and the actual quality of the idea (5%). The Project Manager maintained his view that Idea 2 could not improve any of the identified issues. The Leapp team considered that the adoption of the 'Jenkins's tune-up' could improve the resolution of issues by 38% more than they expected. Once again, both parties did not agree on a potential resolution due to holding different views and perspectives on what might work. It was important, in this context, that evaluations were conducted to generate factual inputs into the decision-making process. It was vital that informed decisions were made rather than making decisions based on assumptions and feelings. It should also be noted that both parties held different perspectives, for example, based on customer expectations (Project Manager) and the views of software or system developers (Leapp team). The target values for both Idea 1 and Idea 2 were initially set at 75%, and according to the Leapp team only

Table 8.10 Difference between Quality of Generated Ideas and Proof of concept

Baseline	Quality of Generated Ideas	Proof of concept	Variance
Idea 1	71%	59%	−12 pp
	64%	59%	−5 pp
Idea 2	0%	0%	0 pp
	50%	88%	+38 pp

Idea 2 met this condition. Although each idea contained sufficient benefits to be considered before deciding whether to adopt the idea, it was ultimately up to the Project Manager to make the final decision.

G2R01—Milestone/Deadline
The purpose of this metric was to measure whether the idea development stage was performed in a timely manner. An initial milestone was agreed and set for the completion of the Idea Development Stage. The outcome of the applied metric met expected results.

G2R02—Total cost of the Idea Development Stage
This metric provided evidence of the actual cost associated with the implementation of Stage 2 (Idea Development). The total cost for the idea generation phase was calculated based on actual time spent during this phase, measured by multiplying hours/days spent by Full Time Equivalents (FTE) and the average hourly rate used within Red Hat at associate/senior leadership level. It was then possible to cost the total amount of work conducted against the financial limit (CZK 200,000) set by Red Hat for this Stage. The total budgeted cost for this Stage did not exceed the limit, on the contrary, the total amount spent was well below the budgeted cost (Table 8.11). The iScorecard team had the responsibility of ensuring that the budget was not exceeded. This was achieved by conducting regular financial performance reviews.

> Note: We applied average weekly labour costs (includes salary and social/health insurance) for confidentiality reasons. In your project you should apply the actual business staff costs to calculate 'actual' costs.

8.7.3 Stage 3: Implementation

The implementation phase demonstrated that generated ideas worked as expected within the CI process. In contrast to Stage 2 (Idea Development) when a lot of exploration and testing was conducted, this Stage was concerned with putting the adopted theory into practice. An important and essential activity often associated with this Stage was the need to maintain control and communicate well with all parties involved. Appropriate metrics fit for their intended purpose for use in this Stage were developed and subsequently selected. This enabled the iScorecard team to record and monitor relevant data from Red Hat to verify if the adopted idea was compliant or non-compliant with the current CI process used in Red Hat. One

Table 8.11 Total actual cost for the Idea Development Stage

Baseline	FTE	Average weekly costs (CZK)	Costs (CZK)
iScorecard	1.85	16,500	30,525
Red Hat	1.19	19,500	23,156
In total			53,681

Table 8.12 Metrics for Gate 3

	Metric number/name	Target
Inputs	G3IO1—Work Effort for Given Tasks	iScorecard max. 1.6 FTE Red Hat max. 0.8 FTE
	G3I02—Senior Management Commitment	Min. 1 from CI team Min.1 from Leapp or Red Hat team
Process	G3P01—Number of Meetings/Calls Within the Innovation Project	Min. 1 at inception + 1 within stage
Outputs	G3O01—Number of Change Requests Relating to Proof of Concept	Radical max. 1 Enhancement max. 2
Results	G3r01—Milestone/Deadline	28th October 2019
	G3R02—Total Cost of Implementation Stage	Maximum 300,000 CZK

important aspect of this approach was to check, for example, if earlier rejected ideas could perhaps still be considered and implemented, based on collecting and analysing new data that provided new insights. Each generated project output was checked for quality and measured to see if it met all the criteria for proceeding to Stage 4. Like the other Stages, the outcomes from Stage 3 (Implementation) were measured (Table 8.12) at the end of two sprints that each lasted for 2 weeks (4 weeks in total).

G3IO1—Work Effort for Given Tasks
This metric measured how productive engaged human resources had been to support the successful roll-out of the concept of Innovation Scorecard within the CI process at Stages 1 and 2. This metric, as part of Gate 1 and 2 activities, measured the time individual team members spent on project related activities, expressed in Full Time Equivalent (FTE) terms (Table 8.13). The target value for this metric was to reach 0.35 for Red Hat and 0.8 for the iScorecard team. It should be noted that the FTE used in this metric was slightly distorted by associated and related time spent on a component known as 'Linter'. This component was related to work conducted in association with CI project extension work for both the Travis and Jenkins platforms. This was an important change in terms of actual efforts required to complete all planned work in a timely manner. This was difficult to achieve for some reasons.

The Leapp Team, during the first two sprints, spent 1 h (0.0125 FTE) checking platform issues relating to Travis. This slight diversion lasted 1 h for each sprint. The first sprint for the other platform known as Jenkins meant that the Leapp team needed to perform so-called 'base of infrastructure stabilization' activities. This involved the correction of regular errors. The second sprint required even more time (24 h or 0.3 FTE). This included changing end to end testing that did not work as needed and rearranging testing that was appropriate and fit for the intended purpose. An unexpected situation arose during the planned third sprint in the form of an external intervention. This intervention included a radical change that allowed the Red Hat to migrate the entire CI process to another cluster (the system on which Jenkins operates). There was no way to prevent intervention, the only compromise they

Table 8.13 Work Effort for Given Task

Baseline	1. Sprint	2. Sprint	3. Sprint	4. Sprint	5. Sprint
Leapp Team	0.06	0.31	External	0.30	0.70
Red Hat team	0.00	0.00	Intervention	0.00	0.10
Leapp PM	0.00	0.00		0.002	0.05
In total	0.06	0.31	0.00	0.302	0.35
Red Hat summary	1.022				
Team Leader	0.30	0.25	0.05	0.05	0.20
Professor	0.10	0.20	0.00	0.00	0.10
Student	0.20	0.22	0.05	0.05	0.20
In total	0.60	0.67	0.10	0.10	0.50
iScorecard summary	1.970				

could achieve was to shift the deadline from weekly to monthly. The fourth sprint involved the migration of an existing cluster (backing up the resource cluster, migrating the backup data and then restoring the data to a target cluster) to a new cluster. This took the Leapp Team 24 h (0.30 FTE).

The intervention was completed during the fifth sprint. This took the Leapp team another 48 h (0.6 FTE) and an additional 8 h by the Red Hat team (0.10 FTE). Once the fourth and fifth sprints were completed, there were still many errors in the infrastructure that caused system blackouts. After each blackout, the help of an outsourcer was required to detect errors, correct them, and provide information on how to resolve the problem in the future. However, even this solution did not prevent the blackouts from happening again after a few days. The summary (Table 8.13) shows that the required FTE values had not been reached. This stage took more time than expected as a direct result of unpredictable intervention. It was Red Hat's intention to maintain the performance quality of the Jenkins platform before the intervention happened to avoid further financial spending.

G3I02—Senior Management Commitment

This metric measured how many senior managers (who supported the innovation project during previous stages and made final 'Go' decisions), were still actively participating in the Implementation Stage. This metric partially fulfilled the set goal to ensure that support for the project was provided and maintained within Red Hat. The target measurement value for this metric was set up to measure if at least one senior management Red Hat team member was still supporting the project after they made a 'Go' decision during the Initial Stage of the project. This metric was executed after each two sprints (monthly). Following an analysis, it was confirmed that at least one of the two project managers involved in this process, were continuing to support the project. The first project manager, who managed the entire CI process from the beginning, continued to support the implementation phase, in which both ideas were tested. The second project manager appeared not to support the ongoing project. On the contrary, his intervention caused many problems in the third, fourth and fifth sprints (already discussed previously).

Table 8.14   Number of meetings/calls within the Innovation Project

	Idea 1: Travis		Idea 2: Jenkins		Intervention	
Baseline	Inception	Within Stage	Inception	Within Stage	Inception	Within Stage
Meeting	2	2	0	0	0	5
Telephone calls	0	0	0	0	0	0
Conference calls	0	0	0	2	0	0
E-comm	0	0	2	2	3	10
Summary	2	2	2	4	3	15

G3P01—Number of Meetings/Calls within the Innovation Project

This metric measured the number of meetings and/or telephone/conference calls held/completed during the CI Innovation Project (Table 8.14) to ensure that relevant project information and progress reports were produced for sharing between the Red Hat Project Manager, the CI team and the iScorecard team. The aim of this metric is to check that clear task responsibilities and commitments to complete these were in place within the project and that support for and awareness of the Innovation Project was maintained within Red Hat. It was agreed with Red Hat that a minimum of one meeting should be held before the Implementation Stage began and one meeting during the Implementation stage.

It appeared that people who worked in IT and Software Development preferred to communicate by electronic means such as a so-called 'ticketing system'. The reason for this was that they did not wish to be interrupted. They needed to focus their attention, without interruption, on the tasks ahead. They viewed interruptions to be interventions that they saw as 'errors in the program', perhaps regarding these as 'we have done something wrong'. Communication levels during the first two ideas' work activities (including Travis and Jenkins) were relatively low as the work was conducted in accordance with the project plan. This changed as soon as interventions occurred. This generated a need for increased communications between members of the Leapp team. Most communications took the form of face-to-face meetings and electronic means. The Jenkins platform had to be migrated to a new 'cluster' as mentioned before, without causing any major concerns or issues. This explained the need to communicate more to avoid these problems.

G3O01—Number of Change Requests Relating to Proof of Concept

It is essential to manage any change requests in a controlled manner to maintain project control. Therefore, this metric was developed to measure how successful change requests were managed and controlled by the Leapp team and make recommendations how to keep change requests to an absolute minimum. This was an important approach. Change requests, in any project, can occur at any time during the life cycle of the project. To make sure proper control over these change requests was exercised, it was essential to control this process.

The set metric target values set were based assuming that no more than five change requests would be received during this stage. It was further assumed that this would include one request for a major or substantial change and five requests for minor changes. Three change requests only were recorded during this whole stage. The first two requests for change were received during the first and second sprints. These were essential as they related to improving the functionality of the Jenkins platform. The first change requested a 'stabilization of the underlying infrastructure' and the second change request requested changes to the 'end to end' testing process as the initial tests did not produce the desired test results. It was therefore necessary to revisit the 'end to end' testing by making necessary changes to the test programme to meet the Leapp team's requirements. Some change requirements were relatively easy to roll out and integrate into the existing end to end test process. One change request was quite complex as it demanded some radical changes to the test process, including the overall migration of an existing cluster to another cluster. These changes were 'declassified' as described in metric G3IO1.

G3R01—Milestone/Deadline
This metric measured the timely performance of the implementation stage. An initial milestone for the completion of the Implementation Stage was set. It was difficult to complete the Implementation Stage within these set time and target parameters.

The radical intervention that occurred during this stage produced some negative impact on the CI process that appeared to make the process less efficient and effective after the innovation was integrated. This explained why the iScorecard team did not achieve the set and expected completion time target.

G3R02—Total cost of the Idea Generation Phase
As per Gate 1 and 2, this metric measured the cost of the implementation phase. The total cost for the idea generation phase was calculated based on actual time spent during this phase, measured by multiplying hours/days spent by Full Time Equivalents (FTE) and the average hourly rate used within Red Hat at associate/senior leadership level (Table 8.15). It was then possible to cost the total amount of work conducted against the financial limit set by Red Hat for this Stage. The highest cost associated with the Implementation Stage related to the fifth sprint. The reason for this was that an existing cluster was transferred and then implemented in another cluster to guarantee the desired high-quality level of integrity of the Jenkins platform.

Table 8.15 Total cost of Idea Generation phase

Baseline (CZK)	FTE	1. Sprint	2. Sprint	3. Sprint	4. Sprint	5. Sprint	Summary
Red Hat	1.48	2438	12,187	–	11,782	31,200	57,606
iScorecard	1.97	19,800	21,945	3300	3300	16,500	64,845
In total							122,451

> Note: We applied average weekly labour costs (includes salary and social/ health insurance) for confidentiality reasons. In your project you should apply the actual business staff costs to calculate 'actual' costs.

Stage 3: Summary
Ideas 1 and 2 appeared to be the optimum solutions for fixing the problems identified with the help of the Leapp team and the Project Manager. When some external intervention occurred that caused some significant damage to the overall system infrastructure, it was no longer possible to continue with the smooth operations of the considered Idea 2 as far as the Jenkins platform was concerned. This intervention also impacted Idea 1 (Travis CI). Travis failed to provide key features to address classified problems (described in G1P01). For this reason, ideas 1 and 2 were evaluated as inadequate, implying that they could not advance to Stage 4 and were evaluated as being a 'No Go' decision. In the next section, a new way of solving the CI process issues was considered and introduced to fix this issue. As it was no longer possible to proceed to Stage 4, the CI innovation project was restarted from its beginning—the Idea Generation stage. After carefully considering new conditions for the CI project the decision to use the same metrics for its success measurement was made to keep continuity and data comparability. The next section presents only relevant core information without the need for more tables.

8.7.4 Project Restart Summary

Stage 1: Idea generation (restarted)
The requirements coming from the radical intervention, were a unique opportunity to generate a new idea, namely: '*To transfer the infrastructure work responsibility to another team*' (Idea 3). Idea 3 was evaluated by the project manager and Leapp team. Its assessment was almost identical which confirmed that both parties felt strongly about this.

Stage 2: Idea development (restarted)
A new Quality Engineering (BaseOS QE) team joined the project at this stage. Their main role was to provide technical quality-related advice and services relating to the migration of the existing infrastructure to another team. After three so-called 'sprints', the Leapp team, in cooperation with BaseOS QE, made progress to migrate CI to another team. Much of this work was in relation to so-called 'pull requests' (a method of submitting contributions, for example, in an open software development project when a developer typically asks for an external repository to be considered for inclusion within the main system's repository). It was thus possible to assess if an idea was compatible with the existing work process. During the Idea Development Stage, no intended or unintended interventions were recorded that

would significantly change the CI process. As a result, proof-of-concept of the CI migration to another team/cluster was developed and evaluated by the same criteria as Idea 1 and 2. Therefore, it was possible to compare all three proof-of-concepts and induce relevant information to help determine whether the idea under scrutiny has a positive impact on key stakeholders' expectations. This proof-of-concept achieved 'best results' compared to the other 'proof-of-concepts'. Both the project manager and the Leapp team agreed that the third proof-of-concept would bring the following benefits:

- An improved flexible infrastructure capable of meeting business and technological changes
- A reduced workload
- A reduction in the need for error correction within Jenkins
- Less input knowledge requirements by team members (Jenkins was complicated and required expertise)
- Testing could be conducted from many locations without the need for a hosted service

Stage 3: Implementation (restarted)
At the implementation stage, this process turned out to be much more complicated than Red Hat expected, thus extending the implementation time. Unplanned time spent on 'debugging' the CI process was needed. While this component was not related to the migration of the Jenkins's infrastructure to another team (proof-of-concept three), it was necessary to complete this work to maintain the integrity of the CI process.

It was important for the Leapp team that the Jenkins migration retained all relevant functionalities and that none of these were lost during the migration. Reality was different. The migration did not go as planned. One of the key functionalities could not be migrated to another team. The absence of this functionality forced the Leapp team to spend a considerable amount of their time to fix this problem which had a negative impact on the time available to do their planned work. In addition, two minor requirements for the new CI solution evolved. They were implemented by external teams within forthcoming planned 'sprint' events. The Leapp team acted as 'consultants' and provided appropriate help and support. The final solution was finally deployed just over a year later than originally planned.

8.7.5   Gate 4: Project Post-Implementation Review

The Post Implementation Review (PIR) was an essential tool to identify and record the 'lessons learned' from this project for the benefit of existing as well as future projects to be undertaken by the iScorecard team. The community of practice of project management such as the Association for Project Management (APM, UK) and the Project Management Institute (PMI, USA) consider that the completion of a PIR provides benefits at individual, team, and organisational levels, and is therefore looked upon as being an essential part of effective project management. The PIR was adjusted to cover the CI project's needs, to provide details of how the project was structured, whether it achieved its success criteria, whether it achieved the expected benefits and what led to any shortfall. The iScorecard team included topics such as 'What did not go well' and 'What went well' in the Agenda for the PIR meeting with the Red Hat team.

The PIR was planned to be organised within 2 months of project closure. Unfortunately, because of a busy 'end of the year' and unavailability of one of the main iScorecard team members due to ill health, the PIR was delayed and held later than originally planned. On the other hand, this time lag could be seen positively since the Leapp and iScorecard teams had more time to review and evaluate the project outcomes. The CI project PIR focused mainly on (i) objectives, (ii) deliverables, (iii) scope of the project, and (iv) lessons learned. This set of four objectives of the CI project was achieved. Goal 2 was difficult to assess due to 'scope creep' during the CI implementation. Due to the external intervention within the implementation stage, the project delivered all required outputs but with significant delays. The main lessons learned from this project, as far as the iScorecard Team was concerned, related to improvements in communications.

The iScorecard team had to spend more time explaining details to Red Hat's staff, in sufficient detail, to aid understanding why the application of performance metrics was so important to the overall success of the project.

Case Study 3: Wi-Fi Global Rollout Project

9

9.1 Introduction

Rather than simply following the examples of the first two case studies associated with the overall Innovation Scorecard project in Red Hat, Brno, Czech Republic, we decided to apply a different approach to make for more interesting reading and to provide you with only the fundamental learning outcomes and different process approaches applied during Case Study 3—Global Wi-Fi Rollout. Therefore, the main attention is more on what is most important for you to know about rather than providing detailed accounts as we have done in the previous two case studies. It is for this reason that we will not bombard you with details of how we collected and analyzed all case study data. The approach has been bearing a close resemblance to that applied during the first two case studies so there is no justification for repeating the same process here.

This case study was the most complex and intricate of the three case studies we implemented. It involved working with an international team of project and general managers, and technical teams across many geographies. This project is ongoing at the time of writing this methodology. We are not able to share all details with you due to the project's confidentiality status. Section 9.2 provides a high-level summary of all the main learning points from our three case studies.

9.2 Executive Summary of the Main Learning Outcomes

The following is a summary of the areas we learned from most in the third case study (in order of priority) and where we feel that our Innovation Scorecard made substantial and significant contributions to Red Hat's operational effectiveness.

Operational resilience and response are essential to successful business operations and management across industries, irrespective of geography. These lay the foundations for managing the inner 'workings of the business' so it runs as efficiently and effectively as possible. Our Innovation Scorecard team identified and

© The Author(s), under exclusive license to Springer Nature Switzerland AG 2021
O. Zizlavsky, E. Fisher, *Innovation Scorecard*, Management for Professionals,
https://doi.org/10.1007/978-3-030-82688-8_9

highlighted some operational issues early in the case study. Red Hat's operational team had conflicting work priorities that sometimes prevented them from developing fast and efficient solutions to meet the ever-changing operational requirements of the business. We drew the project manager's attention to this undesirable shortfall. With our help, continued support, and advice, and through the appropriate application of our Innovation Scorecard, the Red Hat team responded positively and adopted our suggested solutions, with the result that the company's operational resilience and response levels improved significantly. This led to reductions in so-called 'lead time' increases, bringing the project back on track. In addition, further potential delivery solutions were created to provide the business with alternative options, in a fast and efficient manner.

Improved team working is generally at the heart of effective management. The Innovation Scorecard team was familiar with the process of forming a group of people into a team that was to work together for the benefit of this case study. This was achieved formally through the introduction and effectiveness measurement of start-up meetings (so called Definition Workshops or Kick-off Meeting), workshops, regular progress review meetings and developing solutions for the team to work together well. Our suggested approaches to increase team member motivation and the resolution of conflicts that had developed between some team members were important.

Measuring how successful considered changes in this area was of paramount importance and produced the desired results. We modified our approach by considering the cultural characteristics of the international team members: different cultures create different working needs.

People's attitudes and behaviours at work formed an important part of measuring how successful our suggested changes in this area had been. Behavioural characteristics are the elements that separate and describe a person's preferred way of acting, interacting and reacting in a variety of situations. Behaviours complement knowledge and experience and are a function of values, beliefs, and identity. We improved the following behavioural characteristics of team members through the appropriate applications of some attitudinal metrics to measure how successful any changes were in this area: attitude, common sense, open mindedness, adaptability, autonomous thinking, being empowered and inventiveness.

Effective communications are an underlying curiosity or desire to know more about things, people, or issues. Striving to obtain more information and not accepting situations at face value, are key traits associated with this behaviour. We designed and applied performance metrics that measured how successful the Red Hat team was in communicating effectively with each other, once suggested process improvement changes were adopted by the team. Results confirmed that communication effectiveness improved significantly, leading to:

- Higher levels of mutual respect and trust amongst team members
- A noticeable reduction in 'assumptions' being made
- Higher levels of team alignment

9.3   Background

Red Hat considered that it was necessary to update and improve the current Wi-Fi facilities across their world-wide property portfolio providing higher levels of flexibility, agility and scale needed for the modern networking area and seamless network automation. The primary business drivers behind this approach were:

- To reduce business overhead costs
- To introduce new technology, such as the Wi-Fi 6 Standard

This was in response to increased demands for reliable wireless coverage. A reliable hardware and artificial intelligence platforms system was one of the considered options. It allowed Red Hat to implement and operate a robust wireless internet coverage environment within these office locations. The company adopted the view that the introduction and roll out of an optimized Wi-Fi system was highly desirable.

In addition to the already mentioned business needs, another trigger point for upgrading their current system was determined by end user dissatisfaction with the quality of their current wireless services. There was also an operational need to simplify so-called 'troubleshooting' and incident resolution to manage reported shortfalls faster, thus saving the business substantial overhead costs. Further benefits were expected in the areas of making better use of self-services, automation, and improvements to so-called application programming interface (API) service management (allowing two applications to talk to each other). The result would be an enhanced delivery efficiency. Previously investigated solutions did not meet the expected outcomes, thus the need for a better workable solution.

9.4   Objectives and the Innovation Scorecard Design

The overall business objectives for case study 3-Global Wi-Fi Rollout were:

- To optimise wireless signal coverage across all Red Hat's offices
- To improve the quality of access points
- To improve services such as connectivity, trouble shooting and analytics (improved resource allocation)
- To improve the end user experience
- To simplify and automate operations for the IT teams

We applied the company's adopted 'objectives and key performance agile goal setting platform' (OKR) to prioritise goals, align teams and break down so-called 'silos' (working in isolation). The previous approach adopted in case studies 1 and 2 focused on the performance concept of 'goal, critical success factors, key performance indicators, metrics and target values.

To achieve our set targets, we considered that the following actions had to be completed to achieve our objectives:

- To produce the associated Global Wi-Fi Rollout Project Documentation that included a project definition, document (PDD), an appropriate communications plan, a master project management plan, an overall project schedule, an associated resource plan and a budget.
- To produce a software and hardware configuration plan that covered the technical equipment needed across all locations
- To produce an inventory of existing equipment and services for all Red Hat offices
- To procure any system requirements required to meet the new Wi-Fi standard

The following Innovation Scorecard stage gate model, based on the original stage gate model design (Part A of the methodology), was designed, developed, and confirmed as most suitable for our case study 3, with the Global Wi-Fi Rollout project manager.

Two so-called 'pilot studies' at two different locations were planned during the idea development stage. This was essential to test that the chosen technical solutions did work. Testing included unit, integration, and user acceptance testing. It was agreed with the technical team that the implementation stage would be put into effect in two rounds, in order of operational priority (Fig. 9.1):

Round 1—Rollout at core and critical sites
Round 2—Rollout at the remaining sites

The following Innovation Scorecard steps were adopted and implemented:

- Round 1: Installation and Validation/Second Visits (Monitoring and Controlling, Deliverables' transition, training, and marketing
- Round 2: Installation and Validation/Second Visits (Monitoring and Controlling, Deliverables' transition, training, and marketing (Fig. 9.2)

9.5 Communication Flow

As you would expect from an important initiative such as this Global Wi-Fi Rollout project, we considered that it was of paramount importance for us to design, develop and put in place an effective communications plan. The iScorecard team, made up of members of Brno University of Technology and an external PM specialist consultant, worked closely with the Red Hat team. The flow of communication (right information at the right time in the right format to the right people) formed an important part of this project.

A good communication flow is a trademark of effective communications. We developed an appropriate communications plan that was fit for our intended purpose. The communication channels in this case study were similar in nature to channels we considered for case study 2 (CI initiative). We placed a higher emphasis on formal

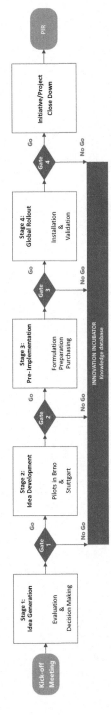

Fig. 9.1 Innovation Scorecard (high-level) stage gate for the Global Wi-Fi Rollout project

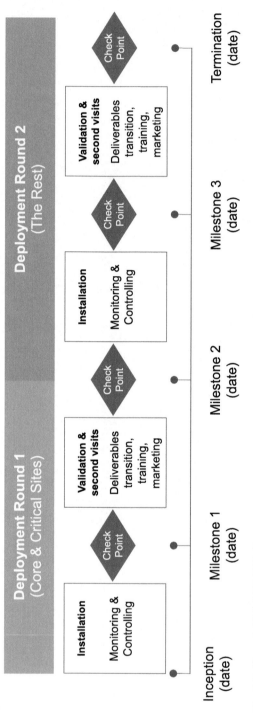

Fig. 9.2 Stage 4: Global Wi-Fi Rollout

communications minimising wasted unnecessary time, money, and energy. The following communication approaches were applied in this project:

- Online meetings (regular and irregular) with Red Hat and the iScorecard Team
- E-mails
- Monthly project progress reports
- Formal and Informal Verbal, Written and Visual Communications
- Google Shared Drive
- Applying effective Information Management to improve effective communications

We considered the following as being essential:

- Active listening and informal communications throughout the project, across all involved and engaged business disciplines: off-line or informal communications lead to closer working relationships than formal communications
- Listening to what team members had to say, paraphrasing to check understanding (particularly important in non-native English-speaking work environments)
- Early detection of issues and then take corrective action to resolve these before they became 'crises'
- Building mutual respect and trust-both develop faster when people can communicate on neutral ground

Typical communication problems experienced during case study 3 work included a lack of communication between team members (not knowing or being aware of progress that had/had not been made), a lack of sharing technical decisions that had been made to all involved team members and the seeking of inputs from experienced team members to fix technical issues. The iScorecard team assisted in fixing these issues by pro-actively engaging with the whole team, suggesting different approaches how to improve these issues, and by monitoring progress made at regular intervals (checking 'before' and 'after' effectiveness levels of communication.

9.6   Applied Metrics

We considered that the third case study provided us with an opportunity to review previously applied metrics (case studies 1 and 2) and to develop more appropriate metrics for this complex and challenging initiative. Performance metrics are applied in business to measure behaviour, business operations and performance. Data is usually produced, collected, analyzed and evaluated, within set parameters, to provide evidence of the achievements of business goals.

Once Red Hat achieved internal technical solution sign off, we produced the following draft list of potential metrics. These included very specific and detailed targets such as % and 'by when' dates. Our primary focus was on capturing performance metrics that we considered were most important and beneficial to Red Hat. The third case study was our biggest challenge:

1. New equipment cost-benefit analysis to be accurate within 10% of actual results (Procurement).
2. New equipment (Wi-Fi) works properly when made available to users (95% of the time).
3. All purchased equipment is compatible with existing S/W and H/W 100% of the time.
4. Ensure new S/W and H/W are operational within 7 days of receipt or in accordance with agreed upon project schedule.
5. Ensure complete documentation and cabling/wiring plans are up to date 100% of the time.
6. Achieve a minimum 30% operational system efficiency by 31 December 2021/ 31 March 2022.
7. Co-ordinate end-user training so all staff are fully conversant within 1 week of going 'live', in accordance with the project roll-out schedule for all 57 locations.
8. Apply the appropriate testing type (unit, integration, user acceptance) for each phase of the system development cycle and achieve 100% compliance.
9. Input of appropriate test data to test the system, with fewer than five entry errors.
10. Categorise system defect so that any potential showstoppers are addressed before minor problems arise.
11. Document results so that testing progress can be determined: timeliness, defects found, number of defects resolved, number of defects retested.
12. A 40% efficiency improvement achieved to simplify and automate operations for IT staff.
13. Target performance metrics:
    a. Improved user experience +35%
    b. Increased revenue +25%
    c. Analytics to improve resource allocation +25%
    d. Asset Optimisation +35%
14. Manual troubleshooting v automated wireless operations: achieved a 35% saving within 12 months of the completed installation (June 2023)
15. Cost savings compared to old system: achieved a 30% saving by June 2023.
16. Wi-Fi performance and reliability: achieve a 25% improvement change compared to old system by June 2021.
17. API: achieve interaction with a separate S/W component or source and achieve a 25% improvement by June 2022.
18. 95% new Wi-Fi Quality Assurance achieved by June 2022.
19. Pre and post implementation metrics:
20. Key Wireless Criteria: Time to connect, capacity, coverage, and throughput. Consider Service Level Expectations (SLE) such as Visibility of this (95%) plus any potential financial metrics expressed in $.

21. Maximise Wi-Fi User experience and achieve a 30% improvement, by June 2022.
22. Minimise IT support costs (before and after):
    a. 25% Attempts
    b. 25% Users
    c. 25% Access Points

The Innovation Scorecard team suggested that the following short list of most appropriate metrics should be adopted by Red Hat (subsequently agreed by the Red Hat project manager). We focused on only those metrics that would provide the highest level of 'business return' if adopted, across some initiative work environments. Some detailed measurements have been omitted due to business 'confidentiality' requirements. We are not going to provide tables/diagrams for these metrics as these were almost identical to those presented in case studies 1 and 2. This is just a high-level overview (for complete list of metrics see Appendix):

- Substantial reduction in operational overhead costs
- Teamwork effectiveness
- Reduction in project sign off process
- Clear roles and responsibilities for all team members
- Improve vendor management approach
- Improve milestone delivery capability

In addition, we suggested that Red Hat should focus on answering the following business questions:

- To what extent are our investments in innovation generating a return (ROI)?
- To what extent is our operating equipment effective (overall equipment effectiveness)?
- How well are we satisfying our users' experiences (savings levels due to improvement efforts)?

9.7   Final Thoughts and Suggestions

1. Clearly identify what the scope of work includes. Without these detailed requirements, it is very difficult and often time consuming to develop appropriate and realistic performance measurement metrics.
2. Engage team members as early as possible and encourage people to get actively involved, by asking for their opinions and inputs and openly showing that you value these. It is not always possible to take all views of all people into consideration but showing that you care about what others think 'goes a long way' to move things forward.

3. Use your influencing skills to good effect is a pre-requisite for managing key stakeholders in any initiative/project. Consider the benefits for the other person, aiming for co-operation and mutual gain (win-win) in an authentic and genuine way. Successful influence is a long-term process, it must be sincere to avoid failure. It is important that people are 'committed' and not just 'compliant'.
4. Risk management is an integral part of initiative/project management. Consider people risks in the context of this innovation scorecard concept, plan for their mitigation, thus de-risking the initiative/project from a people perspective.
5. Manage the different involved parties in the initiative/project as best as you can. Groups of people often have their own separate aims which at some point 'collide' or 'diverge' from the initiative/project. Ensure that the team works as one team, irrespective of their operational diversity. The art of managing these people conflicts is to channel these conflicts so that the result is positive, preferably synergistically so, rather than destructive.
6. Showing cultural competence and awareness in a truly international and cross-cultural team is essential for working effectively. People from different cultures view concepts differently but only from a different angle. Their views are not necessarily right or wrong, just different. To manage people effectively at international level, initiative owners/project managers need to understand what the various trends, sequences and traditions are for the people they work with.

9.8   Main Lessons Learned

The following is a summary of the main lessons learned from the Post Implementation Review (PIR) we conducted with the Red Hat team (Gates 1–3 only). This initiative/project is still ongoing at the time of writing these notes so not all the adopted Gates of the Innovation Scorecard process will be covered.

A PIR is normally completed at the end of an initiative/project but can also be conducted at the end of each process Gate. The advantage of holding the review at the end of each Gate: any lessons learned can be applied immediately to avoid a duplication of mistakes made. The PIR aims to evaluate whether the set and agreed initiative/project objectives have been achieved, how well the initiative/project has been managed, what lessons have been learnt for the future and any actions that need to be taken to optimise initiative/project benefits. Operational hand-over to Business as Usual (BAU) teams is normally included in any PIR if needed.

So, what went well, what did not go so well and what should be done differently in future? Here is a summary of the main PIR outcomes:

What went well:

- The collaboration between the IT network and the workplace technology teams, such as work preparation and installation, communications, and knowledge sharing.
- Fast and efficient production of estimates and quotes in the areas of Network and Wi-Fi hardware.

- High quality production of all initiative/project documentation
- Global integration of structured cabling and Wi-Fi integration

What did not go so well?

- Documentation feedback and approval was often delayed.
- Delivery time scales for the supply of semiconductors.
- Excessive hardware lead times.
- Some firmware limitations such as switches.

What should we do better in future?

- Improved handover (support and maintenance).
- Clear and unambiguous roles and responsibilities of people.
- Standardize IT room cross-connects.
- Standardize IT Network topology.
- Conduct regular discussions with teams to avoid making assumptions.
- Empower team members more so they can engage more in making policy decisions that relate, for example, to network architecture standards.
- Improve operational resilience and response.

Appendix A: Project Action List

Author	
Date	
Version	
Today's date	

Action List

No.	RAG Status	Date	Detail	Owner	Planned completion	Actual completion	Comments
1							
2							
3							
4							
5							
6							
7							
8							
9							
...							

O. Zizlavsky, E. Fisher, *Innovation Scorecard*, Management for Professionals,
https://doi.org/10.1007/978-3-030-82688-8

Appendix B: Contents of Initiative/Project Definition Document (PDD)

Background	Initiative/Project Background
Objectives	Goals/Objectives
Scope	In Scope Out of Scope
Work Breakdown, Organisation and Resource Requirements	WBS (Sect. 5.5) Resource Plan: – Equipment, people, and costs
Milestones and Major Deliverables	Milestone and Deliverable Lists
Management System	Meetings Reporting Schedules Change Control
Assumptions, Constraints and Dependencies	
Issues & Risks	Issues Risks
Immediate Actions	
Attendees at PDW	

© The Author(s), under exclusive license to Springer Nature Switzerland AG 2021   147
O. Zizlavsky, E. Fisher, *Innovation Scorecard*, Management for Professionals,
https://doi.org/10.1007/978-3-030-82688-8

Appendix C: Status Report

© The Author(s), under exclusive license to Springer Nature Switzerland AG 2021
O. Zizlavsky, E. Fisher, *Innovation Scorecard*, Management for Professionals,
https://doi.org/10.1007/978-3-030-82688-8

Initiative/Project Number:	Initiative/Project Name:
Initiative/Project Manager:	
Reporting Period:	
Initiative/Project Status: GREEN YELLOW RED (delete as appropriate)	

Budget:	Planned Percent Complete:
Actual Spend:	Actual Percent Complete:
Variance:	Variance:

Accomplishments:

Upcoming tasks/milestones:

Issues / Risks:

Prepared by:	Date:
Approved by:	Date:

Appendix D: Measurement Inspiration for Gate 1—Idea Generation

Inputs	Funding availability
	Individual networking skills
	Knowledge depth
	Number of incoming proposals from different sources
	Number of patents or prototypes further developed based on existing patent portfolio
	Number of, and time between, collection activities focused on specific external stakeholders (different types of users, customers, competitors, owners, public authorities, etc.)
	Percentage of R&D budget that is non-internal
	Quality IT infrastructure to support interest groups
	Quality of resources allocation process
	Research agreements with partners
Process	Innovation and creativity workshops
	Longitudinal change of proposal such as to see peaks after presentation activities)
	Number of initiatives/projects based on ideas from external stakeholders
	Number of workshops with customers on future needs
	Number of, and time between, activities of presenting the work of the innovative team
	Number of, and time between, activities of systematic idea generation
	Participation of suppliers in stage gate process
	Quality of development innovation process
	Quality of external collaborators
	Quality of planning systems
	Quality of training programs
Outputs	Alliances to further develop ideas
	Employee commitment
	Employee suggestions
	Funds committed to innovation
	Change in core competencies
	Improvement in knowledge stock
	Investment in new projects
	Map of upcoming innovations to the market
	Percentage of growth covered by innovation
	Quality of ideas funded
	R&D staff turnover
Results	Actual versus budgeted costs for planning and knowledge management
	Costs of developing and maintaining infrastructure
	Effort spent in giving feedback

(continued)

© The Author(s), under exclusive license to Springer Nature Switzerland AG 2021
O. Zizlavsky, E. Fisher, *Innovation Scorecard*, Management for Professionals,
https://doi.org/10.1007/978-3-030-82688-8

Elapsed time from proposal to feedback
Expected sales from incremental innovations against competitors
Expected sales from radical innovations against competitors
Change in revenue per employee
Number of submitted proposals from people with rejected proposals (it is important that people continue to give proposals even if not all ideas become projects)
Percentage of sales from ideas originated outside
Percentage of sales together with partners

Appendix E: Measurement Inspiration for Gate 2—Idea Development

Inputs	Amount and quality of customer data acquired related to innovation
	Free time allowances for R&D employees
	Market and technology research resources
	Number of experienced innovation team members
	Number, complexity and size of competitors, customers, partners, and suppliers
	Objectives for innovation efforts clearly communicated to senior managers and employees
	Percentage of performance measures and rewards aligned and linked to innovations
	Quality of information for innovation
	Quality of IT infrastructure
	Success of ideas passing through selection and execution processes
	Time dedicated to innovation
Process	Alignment between innovation strategy and resource allocation
	Cost, development time, delivery time, quantity, and price of products and services offered
	Estimated project effort
	Innovation contribution to R&D projects in progress
	Number of terminated/unsuccessful initiatives/projects (a certain degree of risk-taking is good)
	Percentage of innovation efforts devoted to radical, semi-radical, and incremental innovation
	Portfolio balanced over time, returns, risk, and technologies
	Product platform effectiveness
	Rate and quality of experimentation
	Reduction in new product/process development time/cost within target sales/profits
	Subjective assessment of project risk (feasibility, technical challenge, etc.)
Outputs	Estimated lead time to market launch of project results
	Number of projects with future customer or new market relevance
	Percentage of innovation projects outsourced
	Percentage of sales from new products
	Potential loss (alternative cost) of not selecting a project (worst-case scenario)
	Projected residual income
	Projected sales growth
	R&D productivity
	Ratio of short-term and long-term projects
	Residual income growth
	Sales growth

(continued)

O. Zizlavsky, E. Fisher, *Innovation Scorecard*, Management for Professionals, https://doi.org/10.1007/978-3-030-82688-8

Results	Customer profitability
	Customer satisfaction with innovation activities
	Frequency of repeat customers
	Margin of product and services offered to customers
	Market share
	New customers gained through innovation
	Number of customers through existing products/services who buy new products/ services
	Number of new customers of new products/services who go on to buy existing ones
	Number of new product and service lines introduced
	Profitability of innovation operations
	Revenues generated through innovation efforts

Appendix F: Measurement Inspiration for Gate 3—Innovation Preparation

Inputs	Budget allocation for innovation activities
	Distribution of team members' background, experience, age, and gender
	Estimated remaining investment needed to implement innovation in real products
	Number of competences that are mastered within the team
	Number of process changes which are considered significant improvements
	Number of projects which shift from innovation to normal development
	Project resources (effort, budget, etc.)
	Share of prototype construction which can be reused directly in normal product development
	Share of total effort spent on creative work compared to, such as administration
	Subjective assessment of how well strategic competence areas are covered
	Time allocation devoted to each team member's own proposal
Process	Implementation of new organizational method
	Involvement in the innovation processes
	Lead time per initiative/project
	Level of communication and information flow
	Level of coordination among R&D, marketing, and production units
	Number of projects each team member has managed or participated in
	Share of budget on outsourced projects
	Subjective assessment of the benefit of each process change
	Subjective assessment of the effectiveness of innovation assessment methodology
	Time between deadlines for each project member
	Work environment and relations with co-workers
Outputs	Average development cycle time stages
	Average expenses for innovative activities
	Degree of match between the R&D budget and the objectives set
	Degree of match between the resources deployed and R&D results achieved
	Degree of success in keeping costs to budget
	New products approved/released
	Number of implemented process improvement proposals
	Number of projects per year, number of people involved per project
	Percentage of innovation projects abandoned before their end
	R&D expenses as percentage of sales
	Team-work effectiveness
Results	Average cost of each finished project
	CAPEX
	Cost reduction (derived from innovation initiatives/projects)

(continued)

Monetary rewards for achieved personal and group goals achieved
Monetary rewards for patent proposals
OPEX
Optimization of the use of capital (human and material)

Appendix G: Measurement Inspiration for Gate 4—Innovation Execution

Inputs	Budget percent allocated for innovation effort
	Number of collaboration activities with internal and external stakeholders
	Number of end users of released product features that originate from the team's work
	Number of changes requested which originate from the team's work
	Number of released product features impacted by the team's work
	Number of results from the team accepted by product planning (or other stakeholders)
	Percentage of innovation projects outsourced
	Performance-based compensation linked to innovation success
	Product uniqueness
	Success of ideas passing through selection and execution processes
	Time dedicated to innovation
Process	Alignment between innovation strategy and resource allocation
	Cost, development time, delivery time, quantity, and price of products and services offered
	New product acceptance rate
	Number of gateway returns
	Percentage of innovation projects that respect the cost and outputs planned
	Portfolio balanced over time, returns, risk, and technologies
	Product and process quality score
	R&D productivity
	Rate and quality of experimentation
	Reduction in new product/process development time/cost
	Share of initiative/project effort spent on internal marketing
Outputs	Achievement of quality and time objectives
	Brand image
	Customer acceptance
	Customer satisfaction improvement
	Enlargement of product variety
	General quality of work undertaken in innovation activities
	Market share growth
	Percentage of projects that directly involve the customer
	Percentage of sales from new product
	R&D efficiency (time to market)
	Sales growth
Results	Break even time
	Customer profitability
	Margin of product and services offered to customers

(continued)

New customers gained through innovation
Number of customers through existing products/services who buy new products/services
Number of new customers of new products/services who go on to buy existing products/services
Number of new product and service lines introduced
R&D value creation in commercialisation stages
Return on capital employed
Turnover from and to R&D units

Appendix H: Gate 5 Paper

Initiative/Project Name:		Number:
Strategic Intent:		Issue:
Summary of Initiative/Project Objectives:		
Sponsoring Division:	Sponsor:	
Owner:	Senior Manager:	
Initiative/Project Manager:	Date Raised:	

Document Checklist (where applicable)

Description	Reference	Issue	Date	Author	Approved
Proof of Concept Verified					
User Acceptance Testing Completed (where appropriate)					
Post Implementation Review Report					
Issues and Risks Handover					
Outstanding Actions Handover Completed					
Action Plan for Uncompleted Deliverables					

© The Author(s), under exclusive license to Springer Nature Switzerland AG 2021   159
O. Zizlavsky, E. Fisher, *Innovation Scorecard*, Management for Professionals,
https://doi.org/10.1007/978-3-030-82688-8

Initiative/Project Closedown					
Why is the initiative/project being closed?					
Lessons to be Learnt:					
Comments:					
Recommendations					
				Signature	Date
Project Review Board/Initiative Sponsor	Approve	Reject	Rework		

Change History			
Issue	Raised By	Date Raised	Reason for Revision

Appendix I: Initiative/Project Metric—Costs

INITIATIVE/PROJECT METRICS-COSTS	
Strategic Intent:	
Initiative/Project Name:	
Number:	
Manager:	
Sponsor:	
Date:	
Last Gate passed:	

Costs

	Planned Costs A	Actual Cost B	Percentage Variance to Baseline Schedule $(B - A) / A * 100$
Internal Resources	Man-days	Man-days	%
Capital Equipment	£	£	%
Supplier	£	£	%

Comments on Costs

Guidelines

- Cost metrics should normally be recorded at Gates 1–5, as well as at other key milestones in the initiative/project, especially where there are contractual milestones.
- This form to be initially completed at Gate 1 and at Gates 2–4 thereafter.

Appendix J: Initiative/Project Metrics— Timescale

INITIATIVE/PROJECT METRICS-TIMESCALES	
Strategic Intent:	
Initiative/Project Name:	
Initiative/Project Number:	
Manager:	
Sponsor:	
Date:	
Last Gate passed:	

Timescales

Sponsor's Original Target In-Service Date	Baseline Schedule In-Service Date	Actual In-Service Date
Planned Initiative/Project Duration from Gate 3 to In-Service Date in Baseline Schedule (where appropriate) A	Actual Initiative/Project Duration from Gate 3 to In-Service Date B	Percentage Variance in Initiative/Project Duration $(B - A) /A) * 100$
months	months	%

Comments on Timescales

© The Author(s), under exclusive license to Springer Nature Switzerland AG 2021
O. Zizlavsky, E. Fisher, *Innovation Scorecard*, Management for Professionals,
https://doi.org/10.1007/978-3-030-82688-8

163

Guidelines

- The baseline schedule is a schedule that is established at Gate 3 and is used as a foundation (baseline) for future planning.
- The sponsor's original target in-service date refers to date when the sponsor originally asked for the 'change' to be in-service when they 'endorsed' the initiative/project.
- The baseline schedule in-service date refers to the date that was committed at Gate 3 for the 'change' to be in-service. This date would have been included in the baseline schedule.
- The project duration that is being monitored above is the elapsed time from Gate 3 approval through to the in-service date. Three metrics are included, the planned duration (as stated on the baseline schedule), the actual duration that took place, and the variance (difference) between these two figures expressed as a percentage.

Appendix K: Initiative/Project Metrics—Change Requests

INITIATIVE/PROJECT METRICS-CHANGE REQUESTS	
Strategic Intent:	
Initiative/Project Name:	
Initiative/Project Number:	
Manager:	
Sponsor:	
Date:	
Last Gate passed:	

Change Requests

	Number of CRs with Major Impact	Number of CRs with Minor Impact	Number of CRs with Trivial or No Impact
Requests to change the requirements			
Changes forced upon the initiative/project (rather than being desirable by the initiative/project team or sponsor)			
Changes resulting from proposed technology failing or not understood			
Changes that resulted in a change to the in-service time			
Changes that resulted in a change to the in-service cost of the initiative/project			
Changes resulting in initiative/project scope:			
Increasing			
Decreasing			
No Change			
Change Requests not implemented			
Total:			

© The Author(s), under exclusive license to Springer Nature Switzerland AG 2021   165
O. Zizlavsky, E. Fisher, *Innovation Scorecard*, Management for Professionals,
https://doi.org/10.1007/978-3-030-82688-8

Comments on Change Requests

Appendix L: Initiative/Project Metrics—Staffing

INITIATIVE/PROJECT METRICS-STAFFING	
Strategic Intent:	
Initiative/Project Name:	
Initiative/Project Number:	
Manager:	
Sponsor:	
Date:	
Last Gate passed:	

Staffing

	Key Staff	Non-Key Staff	Total
Planned Number of Staff **A**			
Actual Number of Staff **B**			
Variance in the Number of Staff *(B − A) / A) * 100*			
Number of Planned Staff Changes			
Number of Unplanned Staff Changes			
Total Number of Staff Changes both Planned and Unplanned, that is Staff Churn (Turn over) %			

Comments on Staffing

Appendix M: End of Stage Review Form

END OF STAGE REVIEW RECORD			
Department Name		Initiative/Project Number	
Initiative/Project Name			
Initiative Owner/Project Manager			
		Date	
Gate Stage			
Decision			
Proceed		Proceed but… See actions below	
Hold See actions below		Close See comments	
Actions			
Comments			
Signatures			
Initiative/Project Manager		Date	
Reviewer		Date	
Approver (Senior Manager)		Date	

Appendix N: Sample Risk Identification Starter Lists

NOTE: Initiative owners/project managers should prepare their own lists appropriate to the initiative/project.

RISK AREA: SPONSOR/CUSTOMER/USER
Sponsor/customer may not be clearly identified
Sponsor may be the wrong person (who has most to lose if the initiative/project fails?)
Sponsor may not understand role
Sponsor is not committed for the duration of the initiative/project
Internal/customer staff are inexperienced or frequently unavailable
Initiative team/project team does not have a good working relationship with internal staff/customer staff
Internal staff/customer does not understand the amount of work required to meet the initiative/project objectives
User/business requirements are not formalised
Requirements of the real end users are different
RISK AREA: TECHNICAL
New technology not previously tried and tested
Staff not experienced in development techniques
Staff unfamiliarity with technology/environment
Test/evaluation facilities inadequate
Capacity inadequate (network, computer)
RISK AREA: INITIATIVE/PROJECT MANAGEMENT
Initiative owner/project manager is not at right competency level for this initiative/project
Roles and responsibilities have not been agreed
Estimates are not based on accurate data
Resources have not been committed by line management
Dependencies have not been agreed
Work Breakdown Structure is not complete/on correct basis
Organisational Breakdown Structure is not robust/effective
Cost Breakdown Structure inappropriate (where appropriate)
Initiative/project staff are not working well as a team
Third party/external suppliers

(continued)

© The Author(s), under exclusive license to Springer Nature Switzerland AG 2021
O. Zizlavsky, E. Fisher, *Innovation Scorecard*, Management for Professionals,
https://doi.org/10.1007/978-3-030-82688-8

RISK AREA: OPERATIONAL

Initiative/project deliverables are difficult to integrate with existing systems or business processes

Supporting infrastructure inadequate

RISK AREA: OTHER

Weather or ground conditions (construction initiatives/projects)

External economic environment (interest rates, taxation, currency exchange rates)

Terrorist activity

Political activity

Industrial disputes

Legal/regulatory considerations

Competitor activity

Internal re-organisation

Strategic re-positioning

Appendix O: Contents of Risk Register

Reference	
Date	
Source	
Last Updated	
Description of Risk	
Owner	
Type	
Probability (H/M/L)	
Impact (H/M/L)	
Area(s) Impacted	
Status	
Due Date	
Date Cleared	
Mitigation Plan Reference	

© The Author(s), under exclusive license to Springer Nature Switzerland AG 2021   173
O. Zizlavsky, E. Fisher, *Innovation Scorecard*, Management for Professionals,
https://doi.org/10.1007/978-3-030-82688-8

Appendix P: Example of Risk Mitigation Plan

RISK MANAGEMENT PLAN				
Department Name		Initiative/Project Number		
Initiative/Project Name				
Initiative Owner/Project Manager				
Sponsor (if applicable)		Date		
Risk Reference		Owner		
Risk Description		Priority		
Action Plan	By Whom	By When		Review
Action				

O. Zizlavsky, E. Fisher, *Innovation Scorecard*, Management for Professionals,
https://doi.org/10.1007/978-3-030-82688-8

Appendix Q: Change Request

CHANGE REQUESTS	
Department Name:	
Initiative/Project Name:	
Initiative/Project Number:	
Initiative/Project Manager:	
Initiative Sponsor/Project Owner:	
Raised By:	
Dept/Org.:	
Change Request No:	
Date:	

O. Zizlavsky, E. Fisher, *Innovation Scorecard*, Management for Professionals,
https://doi.org/10.1007/978-3-030-82688-8

Change Requirement:			
Priority:	High	Medium	Low
Reason/Justification for Change:			
Impact of NOT doing Change:			
Response Required:			

Written Quotation	Analysis Only	Contract Change	Other (specify below):
Date Response Required By:			
Date Decision Required By:			
Other: (Description)			
Request Approved By:			
Initiative Sponsor/Project Owner		Date:	
Initiative Owner/Project Manager		Date:	
Issued to supplier of change			
Department/Org.:			
Name:			
Date:			

Issued to supplier of change: Dept/Org.:			
Other depts/areas (apart from actioning dept) copied on change request such as:			
ENGINEERING		OPERATIONS	
CONTRACTS		LEGAL	
HR		BUSINESS DEVELOPMENT	

Appendix R: Typical Content of a Change Control Register

Reference	
Brief Description of Change	
Raised By	
Date Raised	
Result	
Date Agreed/Rejected	
Comments	
Status	

© The Author(s), under exclusive license to Springer Nature Switzerland AG 2021
O. Zizlavsky, E. Fisher, *Innovation Scorecard*, Management for Professionals,
https://doi.org/10.1007/978-3-030-82688-8

Appendix S: Response to Change Request

RESPONSE TO CHANGE REQUEST
Department Name:
Initiative/Project Name:
Initiative/Project Number:
Initiative/Project Manager:
Initiative Sponsor/Project Owner:
Raised By:
Dept/Org.:
Change Request No:
Date:

Summary of Investigation of Requirement:			
Impact to cost (±£'s)		Impact to Plan (time)	
Impact on resources		Commercial Impact	
Impact Analysis:	High	Medium	Low
Response Given:			
Written Quotation	Analysis Only	Contract Change	Other (specify below):
Other: (Description)			
Response Approved By:			
Line Manager/Supervisor:		Date:	
Initiative Owner/Project Manager:		Date:	
Response Rejected By:			
Line Manager/Supervisor:		Date:	
Initiative Owner/Project Manager:		Date:	
Other:		Date:	
Issued to supplier of change request			
Department/Org.:			
Name:			
Date:			
Issued to supplier of change: Dept/Org.:			
Other depts/areas (apart from actioning dept) copied on change request such as:			
ENGINEERING		OPERATIONS	
CONTRACTS		LEGAL	
HR		BUSINESS DEVELOPMENT	

Authority to proceed with change:			
Initiative Sponsor		Date:	
Project Owner		Date:	
CEO/Director/Senior Manager (if required)		Date:	

Appendix T: Change Review

CHANGE REVIEW
Department Name:
Initiative/Project Name:
Initiative/Project Number:
Initiative Owner/Project Manager:
Initiative Sponsor/Project Owner:
Raised By:
Dept/Org.:
Change Request No:
Date:

Actual Cost (±£/€/$'s)		Actual Impact to Plan	
Assessed By:			
Actual Change Carried Out:			
Was Change successful? (If Not-Brief explanation and resulting Action): Y / N			
Change Tested By:			
Name:		Date:	
Name:		Date:	
Name:		Date:	
Change Closed By:			
Name:		Date:	
Name:		Date:	
Name:		Date:	
Change Sponsor:		Date:	

Appendix U: Action List (CI)

Action list					
No./ RAG	Date	Detail	Owner	Planned completion	Actual completion
1.	28.6.2019	Produce monthly dashboard report	Leader	2.7.2019	2.7.2019
2.	28.6.2019	Produce high level project documents—PDD, Issues and Risks Register, Change Control Process, Project Action list	Leader/ Student	2.7.2019	2.7.2019
3.	28.6.2019	Produce Schedule for the project	Professor	6.12.2019	19.12.2019
4.	28.6.2019	Update the PDD and review it by Red Hat	Leader	5.7.2019	5.7.2019
5.	30.7.2019	Discuss and develop metric for CI project	Leader	31.8.2019	31.8.2019
6.	2.9.2019	Get all research data from Red Hat	Leader/ Student	15.10.2019	18.10.2019
7.	2.9.2019	Write to CEO of Red Hat to get more support	Professor	2.9.2019	2.9.2019

O. Zizlavsky, E. Fisher, *Innovation Scorecard*, Management for Professionals,
https://doi.org/10.1007/978-3-030-82688-8

Appendix V: Risk Register (CI)

Risk Register				
No./ RAG	Date	Detail	Value	Measure
1.	5.8.2019	Red Hat may decide to stop the CI project and restart	The iScorecard team needs to spend more time to restart the project	Will be reviewed monthly
2.	2.9.2019	The key member of Red Hat may leave the company	Project costs may increase	This no longer a risk by 30.11.2019
3.	2.9.2019	The iScorecard team cannot complete all measurements	More time needed and costs may go up	Risk closed. This is now an issue
4.	19.12.2019	The impact of IBM on the availability and commitment of Red Hat stuff	The iScorecard team needs to make more available to get information from RH	Will be reviewed monthly

O. Zizlavsky, E. Fisher, *Innovation Scorecard*, Management for Professionals, https://doi.org/10.1007/978-3-030-82688-8

Appendix W: Issues Register (CI)

Issues					
No./ RAG	Date	Detail	Owner	Planed completion	Actual completion
1.	5.7.2019	Access into Red Hat internal network	Leader/ Student	7.8.2019	7.8.2019
2.	13.8.2019	Lack of research data from Red Hat	Leader/ Student	18.10.2019	
3.	2.9.2019	Problems with shared drive documents	Leader	30.10.2019	30.10.2019
4.	2.9.2019	Current time spent on project by iScorecard team member	Leader	30.11.2019	15.12.2019
5.	19.12.2019	Lack of commitment by Senior Management in Red Hat	Leader/ Professor	31.1.2020	

Appendix X: Original Project Plan (CI)

ID	(i)	Task Name	Duration	Start	Finish	Predecessors
1		Original Red Hat Continuous Integration Project Master Plan	282 days	Mon 6/03/19	Tue 6/30/20	
2		Stage 1: Idea Generation:	43 days	Mon 6/03/19	Wed 7/31/19	
3		Resource Requirements (Red Hat and iScorecard team)	8 days	Mon 6/03/19	Wed 6/12/19	
4		Stakeholder Buy-in	7 days	Thu 6/13/19	Fri 6/21/19	3
5		Work input monitoring	4 days	Mon 6/24/19	Thu 6/27/19	4
6		Managing actions and issues	4 days	Fri 6/28/19	Wed 7/03/19	5
7		Produce initial ideas list	4 days	Thu 7/04/19	Tue 7/09/19	6
8		Clarify RH ownership of work packages	4 days	Wed 7/10/19	Mon 7/15/19	7
9		Produce Gate 1 milestone	4 days	Tue 7/16/19	Fri 7/19/19	8
10		Decision to proceed to Gate 2	4 days	Mon 7/22/19	Thu 7/25/19	9
11		Stage 1 costs	4 days	Fri 7/26/19	Wed 7/31/19	10
12		M 1 milestone	0 days	Wed 7/31/19	Wed 7/31/19	
13			0 days	Wed 7/31/19	Wed 7/31/19	
14		Stage 2: Applied R&D:	43 days	Thu 8/01/19	Mon 9/30/19	12
15		Resource Requirements (Red Hat and iScorecard team)	4 days	Thu 8/01/19	Tue 8/06/19	11
16		Stakeholder Buy-in/approval	4 days	Wed 8/07/19	Mon 8/12/19	15
17		Agree time for reviewing /developing and discussing project work	2 days	Tue 8/13/19	Wed 8/14/19	16
18		Conduct research to develop best practice	6 days	Thu 8/15/19	Thu 8/22/19	17
19		Review inputs against CI project	4 days	Thu 8/22/19	Tue 8/27/19	
20		Red Hat and iScorecard team to conduct final idea review	5 days	Thu 8/29/19	Wed 9/04/19	
21		Check the CI process capability with the final list of ideas	4 days	Thu 9/05/19	Tue 9/10/19	20
22		Check that the final ideas are 'fit for the intended purpose' and meet Red Hat's objectives	3 days	Wed 9/11/19	Fri 9/13/19	21
23		Ensure that all Gate 2 actions have been completed (Gate 3 ready)	3 days	Mon 9/16/19	Wed 9/18/19	22
24		Ideas list and proof of concepts finalised, including QA	4 days	Thu 9/19/19	Tue 9/24/19	23
25		Ensure all work is committed	3 days	Wed 9/25/19	Fri 9/27/19	24
26		Stage 2 costs	2 days	Fri 9/27/19	Mon 9/30/19	

Project: 200509 Red Hat CI Project Master Plan Issue 1 for Tanya	Task	▬▬▬	Project Summary	Inactive Milestone ◇	Summary Rollup	Progress ▬▬▬
	Split	....	External Tasks	Inactive Summary	Manual Summary	Deadline
Date: 5/9/2020 5:14 AM	Milestone ◆		External Milestone ◆	Manual Task	Start-only ⊏	
	Summary		Inactive Task	Duration-only	Finish-only ⊐	

Page 1

Appendix Y: Monthly Progress Report (CI)

 Continuous Integration (CI) Project
Monthly Progress Report

Last Month (December 2019)	This Month (January 2020)
• Completed and submitted the grant application for APM and produced the draft grant application for the PMI (round 1 and 2) • Further contacts with both the APM and PMI regarding publication of our work • The CAFINews paper was published • Chased the APM Project magazine editor regarding the publication of our Project Article • Completed one of the chapters of the final master degree thesis (subject is the iScorecard Project in Red Hat) • Eddie signed a new contract with BUT (1.5 days per week) • Received full support from Ludek Smid for publishing our research articles and for the APM and PMI grant applications	• Planned questionnaire with the Red Hat Leapp team • To develop and complete Idea 3 with Red Hat • Hold more meetings with Red Hat to get all outstanding research data so that the iScorecard team can complete all metrics work and the planned questionnaire with the Red Hat Leapp team • Update the current project schedule once the data from Red Hat has been received • Update the iScorecard shared drive • To complete final review of the PMI grant application • Tana and Ondrej will attend DevConf 2020 • Ondrej has been invited to take part in Red Hat Research Day (a day before DevConf)

Help Required

• Help needed from Red Hat to complete the questionnaire and to provide all outstanding data

O. Zizlavsky, E. Fisher, *Innovation Scorecard*, Management for Professionals, https://doi.org/10.1007/978-3-030-82688-8

Appendix Z: Innovation Scorecard Data Sheet (CI)

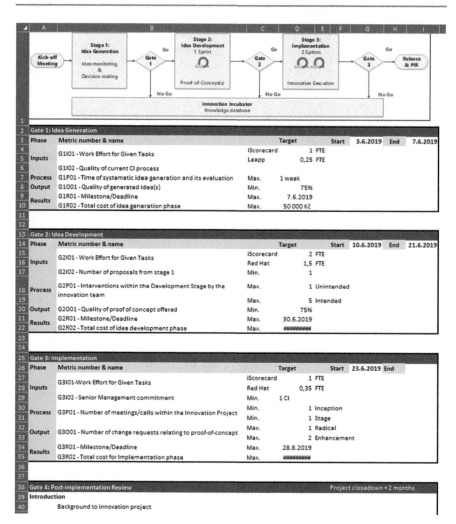

Gate	Gate 2	Phase	Output	Metric name	G2OO1 - Quality of proof of concept offered
Goal	To demonstrate that the CI process adoption has led to improvements within Red Hat in the area of operational performance.				
Definition	Provide proof that the CI process is fit for its intended application within Red Hat.				
Formula	Interviews/questionnaire outcomes from Red Hat operational Leapp PM and Leapp team		Lag/Lead	Lagging	
Data source	consideration		Frequency	At the end of stage	
Data quality	High		Polarity	Min.	
Data collector	Student		Unit type	%	
Data owner	Leapp team + Leapp PM		Target	75%	

Baseline		Idea 1: Migration from Jenkins to Travis CI		Idea 2: Jenkins tune-up	
Problem	Weight	Leapp PM	Leapp Team	Leapp PM	Leapp Team
Unit tests	0,5	100%	100%	0%	100%
Build creation	0,1	0%	0%	0%	75%
End2End tests	0,1	0%	0%	0%	75%
Complexity	0,3	30%	30%	0%	75%
		59%	59%	0%	88%

Appendix AA: Project Definition Document (CI)

CONTINUOUS INTEGRATION

PROJECT DEFINITION DOCUMENT

Document Information:

Author:	iScorecard Team
Date:	30 July 2019
Version:	Final 1.0
Document Ref.:	

Quality Control Sign Off:	
Name:	
Review Date:	

Document Approval:	
Name:	
Role:	
Approval Date:	

© The Author(s), under exclusive license to Springer Nature Switzerland AG 2021   199
O. Zizlavsky, E. Fisher, *Innovation Scorecard*, Management for Professionals,
https://doi.org/10.1007/978-3-030-82688-8

Change History:

Version	Date	Changed by	Changes
Draft 0.1	25 June	Tetyana Shpilka	First Draft
Draft 0.2	27 June	Tetyana Shpilka	Updated after RH meeting
Draft 0.3	28 June	Tetyana Shpilka	Further update
Draft 0.4	08 July	Ondra Žižlavský	PBS, Gantt, time schedule
Final 1.0	30 July	Ondra Zizlavsky	Comments from RH incorporated

Distribution Plan:

Version	Issued to:			
Final 1.0	Marcel Gazdík			
	Vojtech Sokol			
	Ondra Žižlavský			
	Eddie Fisher			
	Tetyana Shpilka			

Introduction: General

Continuous Integration (CI) is a practice used within IT and Software development. Developers integrate code into a shared repository frequently, preferably several times a day. Each integration can then be verified through automated build and test processes. Automated testing is applied regularly in Red Hat. One of the key benefits of integrating regularly is that it is possible to detect errors quickly and locate these more easily. As each change introduced is typically small, pinpointing the specific change that introduced a defect can be done quickly and efficiently. Continuous Integration (Fig. AA.1) is the practice of merging all developers'

Fig. AA.1 Continuous integration and deployment (codeship.com/continuous-integration-essentials)

working copies to a shared 'main line model' (well-established branching model). This usually happens several times a day. It ensures that individual developers who work on code modification, do not get distracted. When integration is combined with testing, continuous integration can enable code to become dependable. **Continuous Deployment** is a strategy for software releases. It is closely related to Continuous Integration and refers to keeping applications deployable at any point in time. This includes being automatically released to a test or production environment provided latest code commit versions have passed automated tests. **Continuous Delivery** is the practice of keeping the codebase deployable at any point in time. Applications must pass automated tests and have necessary configurations before being pushed into production. Development teams then push changes that passed the automated tests into a test or production environment immediately to ensure a fast development loop. (https://codeship.com/continuous-integration-essentials).

Background

The main purpose of the Continuous Integration project is to apply the output of some research in the area of innovation scorecard to a real-life software development project in Red Hat, Brno, Czech Republic (Fig. AA.2). This project forms part of an Innovation Scorecard initiative that has been funded by the Czech Republic Grant Agency. In this context, the Innovation Scorecard system was designed as a part of a project under the Grant Agency of the Czech Republic. The implementation of the Innovation Scorecard will contribute to improving the efficiency, economies of scale (operational level) and the ultimate competitiveness of organizations in the IT industry. This is the second project in a series of projects that forms part of the Innovation Scorecard endeavour. The second project is known as Continuous Integration. The Continuous Integration process (Fig. AA.3) applied by this project uses a web-based open-sourced hosting service for version control known as GitHub. GitHub is a subsidiary of Microsoft. It is mostly used for computer coding. It is about discovering, sharing and building better software. A repository (repo) is a location where all the files for a particular modification are kept. This allows software developers to easily collaborate as they can download a new version of the software, make changes and upload the newest revision. Every developer can see these new changes, download them and contribute. GitHub is used for sharing issues

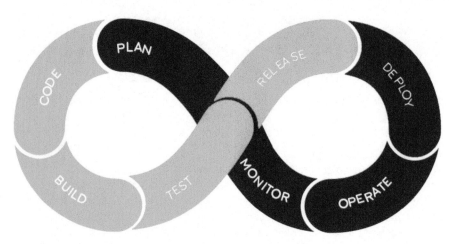

Fig. AA.2 DevOps lifecycle (CI in yellow) (https://medium.com/@gwright_60924/continuous-integration-ci-e81032bb8502)

with other users, for example, what not to use/or what to use. The 'suggester' writes a feature change. When that person is ready to engage their local team, a pull request is started. This shows others the proposed changes, provides an opportunity to discuss them and aids blockage management. Anyone can add new ideas or changes to the existing change. GitHub keeps a record of everyone's contributions, including relevant messages. Once the local team has agreed all changes, everyone will be able to see this. Now developers can benefit from the new idea. Applications are not limited to specific industries. One of the objectives of this project is to improve the current modus operandi, with particular emphasis on process improvement. It is of paramount importance to identify areas of weakness within the process and strengthen these so that higher levels of efficiency and effectiveness can be achieved. The CI process starts by either generating a new code or checking GitHub whether a new code already exists. If a new code exists, this code is obtained from GitHub. If there is no code available, a new code needs to be developed. If yes, GitHub's 'continuous integration started' is updated. The next step in the CI process is to conduct appropriate testing and then update the GitHub status. If test results are positive, the 'Trigger build' process is started including updating GitHub. If the test is negative, GitHub is updated. If build is accepted, then the 'end 2 end' status is 'flagged' to confirm that all is well to proceed. This will trigger the e2e tests. The final step in the CI process is to update GidHub with the e2e tests results.

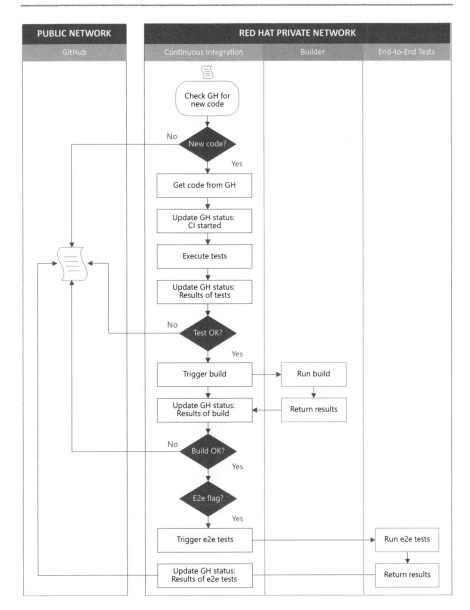

Fig. AA.3 CI process for the Leapp project in Red Hat

Objectives

The considered objectives for the Continuous Integration project are:

* Make the process easy to update and fit for its intended purpose
* Reduce or minimize maintenance
* Improve the speed of managing issues
* Reduce engineering input time

Critical Success Factors (CSFs)

The discussed and agreed Critical Success Factors are:

* Reduce overhead for the Continuous Integration process
* Improve the current development and maintenance modus operandi

Key Performance Indicators (KPIs)

* Reduce maintenance by 20% by 30 June 2020
* Improve Continuous Integration by providing evidence that the process, after innovation, has been followed and applied 90% of the time
* Reduce re-work time for testing and shorten the CI review time by 30% by 30 June 2020

Key Stakeholders

The key stakeholders for the CI project are:

* CI project manager
* CI senior manager

Scope

The scope of work for the CI project was discussed and agreed at the project review meeting with Red Hat on 25 June 2019. The purpose of the meeting was to establish the expected deliverables that Red Hat want the innovation scorecard team to deliver. The review meeting confirmed the in and out of scope requirements for the Continuous Integration project:

In Scope:
- The use of the innovation scorecard concept for all design elements of the Continuous Integration project
- Data collection processes improvement
- iScorecard roll-out in to the Red Hat within the CI project

Out of Scope:
- Technical solutions necessary to improve or change any aspect of the CI project

Constraints

The innovation scorecard team together with inputs from the Red Hat project team identified the following single most important and relevant limitation that could affect successful project delivery:

- Changes in technology that are based on the internal team's approach to these changes, for example, in the service area

Assumptions

- Red Hat will provide the innovation scorecard project team with reasonable access to all relevant and required information
- Red Hat staff will respond to requests for information or meeting attendance within 1 week of the date of the request
- The innovation iScorecard team will remain the same for the duration of the CI project

Risks

Following the CI project review meeting with Red Hat, both parties confirmed that there are no risks currently identified within the CI project.

Reporting

Red Hat confirmed that the innovation iScorecard team needs to submit a monthly project status report in the form of a dashboard report. The content of the dashboard report will cover the following activities:

- Current status (red = serious issue, amber = minor issue and green =all is going well)
- Work delivered this month
- Work planned for the next reporting period

Dependencies

The iScorecard team is dependent on:

- Red Hat to provide Continuous Integration project performance data so that the IScorecard team can conduct an analysis and evaluation of performance metrics
- Support from all Red Hat CI team members

Communications

There will be a continuous communication flow in this project between Red Hat and the Innovation Scorecard team (Fig. AA.4). Regular interactions will take place in the form of face to face, telephone and electronic communications. The Red Hat project manager is in charge of a team of nine people. The Red Hat deputy project manager looks after a team known as the LEAPP team. Red Hat advised that their current team structure could change in line with changing operational requirements. The iScorecard team, made up of members of Brno University of Technology and an external PM specialist consultant, work with the Red Hat Project Managers. All lines of communication follow this hierarchical structure. The flow of communication (right information at the right time in the right format to the right people) forms an important part of this project.

The following communication methods will be applied in this project:

- Meetings (regular and irregular) with Red Hat and the iScorecard Team
- E-mails
- Monthly project progress reports
- Formal and Informal Verbal, Written and Visual Communications
- Workshops, Presentations and Publications
- iScorecard Website

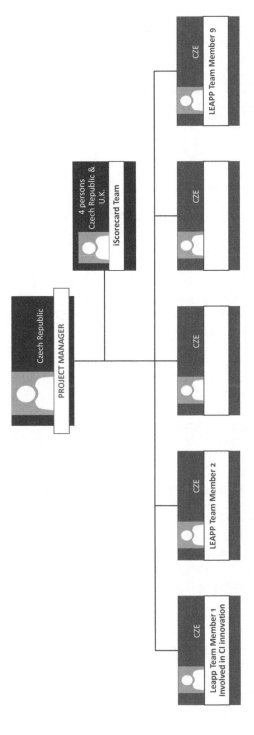

Fig. AA.4 Communication flow diagram for the iScorecard project

Deliverables

The iScorecard Team will deliver the following:

- All relevant project documentation, including objectives, CSFs and KPIs
- iScorecard solution for application in the Continuous Integration process, including innovation stages and gates, appropriate metrics used for innovation evaluation in each gate and the scorecard design
- Data collection
- (Monthly) dashboard reports
- Research paper for international publication/Case study for iScorecard book

Project Schedule, Gantt Chart and Product Breakdown Structure (PBS)

This shows the work that has been planned to be performed within the CI project. Interdependencies between all various activities are shown. Estimates of duration and efforts can then be made as part of the Stage Gate process. A Product Breakdown Structure has been produced to show the various high level activities associated with the Continuous Integration project.

Project Master Plan draft (PDF)
https://drive.google.com/a/vutbr.cz/file/d/130RsjnpOvCR9KyR_s76sZzOg_jWYhkYH/view?usp=sharing

Project Master Plan draft (MS Project)
https://drive.google.com/a/vutbr.cz/file/d/131Ph6as8pTGZa3CMPP2NzAS6GGvklaUt/view?usp=sharing

Product Breakdown Structure (PDF)
https://drive.google.com/a/vutbr.cz/file/d/1-9CuFQx7_eTeSILLT8x-MU2LC9GYB3jh/view?usp=sharing

Product Breakdown Structure (Mind Mapping Software)
https://drive.google.com/a/vutbr.cz/file/d/1-8ZRD7V1Ms7dJsCtVd0egfbVUwe9yLEM/view?usp=sharing

Appendix AB: Applied Metrics (Wi-Fi)

Gate 1: Idea Development		
	Metric number & name	Target
Input	G1I1 Price for licence of current Wi-Fi solution	Stop the increase & reduce
Process	G1P1 Number of various stakeholders involved in this stage (market research and evaluation)	Min X Engineers from Y Depts
	G1P2 Effectiveness of teamwork	n/a
Output	G1O1 Quality of idea(s)	Best ranking
Result	G1R1 Costs	n/a

Gate 2: Idea Development (Pilots)		
	Metric number & name	Target
Input	G2I1 Clarity of strategic objectives	Yes, strategic objective is clear (scale)
Process	G2P1 Collisions with current HW/SW	Max 2 critical, Max 3 medium, max 5 low
	G2P2 End2End Testing	Efficient (Min/Max) number/minutes of tests + results (min. 90% Green)
	G2P3 Effectiveness of teamwork	6 responses
Output	G2O1 Quality of pilot	Acceptance criteria Passed
Result	G2R2 Budget/Costs/time spent on this project	n/a

O. Zizlavsky, E. Fisher, *Innovation Scorecard*, Management for Professionals, https://doi.org/10.1007/978-3-030-82688-8

Gate 3: Pre-implementation

	Metric number & name	Target
Input	G3I1 Roles & Responsibilities	All roles and responsibilities identified
Process	G3P1 Loss Time (not having information from various parties)	Max. XX hours
	G3P2 Vendor management	Best ranking
Output	G3O1 Wi-Fi global Rollout Project Management Plan	All documentation ready
Result	G3R1 Estimated Budget	USD500,000 min

Gate 4: Global rollout

	Metric number & name	Target
Input	G4I1 Project Sign Off Process	To reduce the number of signatures needed for sign off by 30% To reduce the time it takes to get the signatures by 30%
Process	G4P1 Vendor Performance	To ensure that the vendor delivers to time, cost, quality, and specification To monitor vendor capability
Output	G4O1 Milestone Delivery Performance	100% delivery of all milestones To improve milestone delivery capability
Result	G4R1 End Users Satisfaction with New Wi-Fi Solution	Increase in user satisfaction by 25% To reduce service level issues by 20%

Glossary of Terms

APM BOK Association for Project Management Body of Knowledge
BAU Business as Usual
BOSCARD Background, Objectives, Scope, Constraints, Assumptions, Risks/ Reporting, Deliverables
CI/CD Continuous Integration/Continuous Development
CEO Chief Executive Officer
CR Change Request
CSF Critical Success Factor
FTE Full Time Equivalent
HR Human Resources
ISO International Standards Organisation
IT Information Technology
KM Knowledge Management
KPI Key Performance Indicator
OKR Objectives, performance indicators, key results
PDD Project Definition Document
PDD Project Definition Document
PDW Project Definition Workshop
PERT Project/Program Evaluation Review Technique
PIR Post Implementation Review
QE Quality Engineer
RAG Red, Amber, Green
ROI Return on Investment
SLA Service Level Agreement
UAT User Acceptance Testing
WBS Work Breakdown Structure

© The Author(s), under exclusive license to Springer Nature Switzerland AG 2021   211
O. Zizlavsky, E. Fisher, *Innovation Scorecard*, Management for Professionals,
https://doi.org/10.1007/978-3-030-82688-8